Let Go

Release the Grip of the Past and Grab Ahold of Your Future

By

Ty Finley

Table of Contents

Dedication

This book is dedicated to my husband, Freddie; your love, friendship, and support over the years have been unparalleled. I love our journey, we've had to let go of a lot, but God has been with us every step of the way. I love you deeply and I am honored to be your wife.

To my children, Timothy and Tiffany; thank you for your support, for your help and for listening to my ideas. I appreciate your laughter and encouragement. I am so proud of you, you both are learning to let go. Remember, I am with you on this journey but most importantly God is with you. I love you both dearly.

To my mother, Anitra; thank you for your friendship, fervent prayers, and for holding up my arms. You have been a great support. I love you more.

To my late grandparents, Dr. Robert and Superintendent Victoria L. Thrash, because you let go of the hurts of your past. God was able to do tremendous things in your life and the lives of generations after you.

Acknowledgements

This book's inception started many years ago. However, two and half years ago, I knew it was time to give birth to it. I would like to thank every person who inspired me during this process. I am the sum total of all I have known, met, let go of, and learned from. I want to acknowledge everyone who played a role of support, whether that be fasting, praying, friendship or encouragement. This book would not be possible without you. I'd like to express my deepest thanks to Team Hopeful Hearts for their friendship and for the reminder that no one is alone on this journey. To all my supporters at Talk Forty To Me, thank you for allowing the blogs to be a starting point for this pivotal moment. A special thank you to Amazon Publishing; Nancy Brown, Editor, and Zara Morton, Project Manager, thank you both for your professionalism and patience. Zara, Tony, Walter, John, Neha, David & Roy and their team you helped bring the vision to life and you are all amazing. Thank you for going above and beyond and helping to finalize this project. Last but not least, I thank God, for without him, nothing in my life would be possible.

About the Author

Ty Finley is a wife, mom, writer, speaker, accountant, encourager, and motivator, but most of all, she is a daughter of the King. Her life has been filled with trials, tests, and countless victories. Ty's goal is to empower and encourage others to overcome in life, sharing the tools she's developed with her walk with God. Her approach with scriptures and real-life examples demonstrate the practicality of the word of God and how it can be applied in every area of one's life.

Introduction

Have you ever felt stuck? Stuck behind heartbreak? Stuck behind a bad decision you made? Stuck in a relationship? Stuck in a bad self-image of yourself? Feeling as though you can't move forward or feeling inadequate because of your past! Today, I am here to tell you that it's okay to lose the grip and let go.

Let go of the comparisons, the shame, the hurt, the pain, the rejection, the betrayal, and move into the life God ordained for you. Move out of the valley of stuck and start journeying again. Soon you will feel the weight lifted off your shoulders. You can run, shout, move freer, and hear God's voice clearer when you start letting go of the baggage that's been holding you back and keeping you down. What you've been holding onto is no good for your future or your health.

Letting Go sounds much simpler than it truly is, I get it! You may have been holding on to the pain for years or what feels like a lifetime, and rightfully so in many instances. Holding on to these things feels like a necessity, it's a protection mechanism. But, holding on keeps you burdened and bogged down, and though you can make progress in your life, it won't be to the full magnitude that God has purposed for you. It's time to let go, release the pain and pressure, and be free.

Hebrews 12:1 tells us to, "…. Lay aside every weight, and the sin that so easily besets us, and let us run with patience the race that is set before us" (KJV).

Holding on is painful, while letting go seems scary. You may have created a safe space of emotional turmoil and baggage. It allowed you to build walls of protection to keep people at bay. However, the very walls you've created to keep others out have become the prison that keeps holding you back. No deep connections can form, and no new life is able to flow continually. That is all going to start changing for you as you understand you hold power to let go.

It will be a continual process. It won't happen overnight. As you make a conscious effort to lay aside the weight and loads that are too heavy, you'll be free to laugh, dream, and love again. The negative, painful loads were never designed for you to carry. Yet, there you've been year after year, relationship after relationship, job after job, still holding on to the pains from your past.

The pains from your past will haunt you if you don't allow them to propel you and transform you into something greater. If you dwell on the injustice and never move, never grow; you will wallow in who walked away, what was done or said, and you will never reach your destiny.

The enemy of your soul would like nothing more than to keep you stuck and weighed down. He does not want you to comprehend your worth and value in God. I know because I've been there.

This book will discuss a portion of my journey of letting go as well as the words of wisdom God spoke to me that will encourage and empower you. God is no respect of persons, and he wants to heal you completely, he wants you free, and he wants you whole.

Through this book, you will find practical ways to deal with the pain of yesterday, release all the bondage of your past, to become all that God has shown you. So, are you ready?

Chapter 1: The Journey of Letting Go

Throughout my life, I've endured many personal storms, or what I'd like to call those thorns in my side. I am certain you can attest to the same. One moment, I am sailing through life just fine, and then one day, I find myself ensuring to stay anchored, trying to have my spiritual life vest on, holding on for dear life, and trying to remain calm during the next storm or prick.

To some, staying calm during a storm sounds as ridiculous as staying calm when there is turbulence on an airplane. Some people are good with it, but others won't rest until the plane stops shaking and when the storm subsides.

As the waves would beat stronger around me, the intensity kept me praying. However, I had to rely on what I already knew when the storm felt like it would never pass, and I couldn't hear the words of others or even my thoughts due to the vehement winds. I have to keep reminding myself that God would bring me through, and God always shows me how to have peace amid the storms of life.

A few years ago, my life changed forever. As a woman, I believe we can have it all. The marriage, the children, the career, the business, the friendships (cause not everyone wants to be married), but we must be honest with ourselves and know when we have taken on too much and when to let go—prioritizing what is most important to us. I strongly believe that we can have it all. ALL is going to be different for each one of us. If what we want aligns with what God wants, it's ours!

If you have or are desiring a family, I admonish you to put your family first, only second to God. Make sure you are taking the time to be a listening ear, not rushing them to hurry so you can go on to the next thing. Ensure that you are enjoying the simple moments of life, like taking a walk with your spouse or children or laughing at a funny video they show you. Take time to build your house and live with intention at the moment with them.

I'm a wife and mom before I am anything else, so my family is always my priority, aside from God. My desire was to always work close to home so I would never miss a school event, award ceremonies, or a basketball game. I had the honor to be a stay-at-home mom and enjoyed that. But when my kids went to school full time, I went back to work too. For eight years, I was blessed to work close to home. The goal was to always work close to home until they both graduated and went off to college. But I wanted more, got ahead of myself (and God), and found an ideal position with a lengthy commute.

In the beginning, the work was great. Then about a year later, I got ridiculously busy. I worked at work, brought my work home, and held and attended meetings when I should've been done for the day, even on my days off. I slowly noticed that I started working from home and on weekends as well, which was always a no-no for me.

Not only was I becoming a workaholic, but I was also neglecting my family, giving them the little bit of whatever I had left. I used my commute time to pray and think and spend some time in silence. Still, I was tired and drained. To top it all off, I neglected one very important person: ME! It was something about this job where I had a hard time saying NO. Never in my life did I have this problem before then nor after. I was not using wisdom by any means.

I would tell myself, do all you can do, learn all you can know, and in two years, you can move up to an even better position, making X amount of dollars. I was climbing a ladder that was not designed for me at that time. Yes, I excelled. Yes, I was gifted. Yes, I had struggles. But this is what I wanted. If there was a project available, I worked on it, either solo or on a team.

Personally, I already had what I felt I wanted in life – family, house, cars, vacations, etc. However, there was much more I wanted professionally, and it came at a cost. I had so much of what I desired in life but noticed I was lacking intimacy. Material things do not fill voids or callings in our lives. Only God can do that. It took wisdom to realize that I needed to realign myself closer to Abba. I needed to trust God's timings and not my own.

On a personal level, my life was suffering. Of course, I had the flexibility and could pick my kids up from school, but I was all over the place. My children were teenagers and were happy that I was so busy I wasn't noticing every detail. We talked, we laughed, and we had dinner together, but I'd have to interrupt to take a call and then find time to do this thing called "sleep." I was on the freeway or at work before they even got up in the mornings. I kept telling myself, "Just two more years."

My husband would tell me I was doing too much, working too far, working too many hours, and taking too much crap. He traveled a lot for work during this time, and though he didn't complain, he'd say one of us must work close to home for the kids. I would always say give me two more years.

Sure, I had plans for myself, but God had other plans for me. Two more years wouldn't do. I could feel the pressure. I knew I needed to be there for them. "NOW!!!!!! Two years will be too late," I told myself. I thank God I didn't spend many years down this road, but it was long enough. I needed to humble myself; and had a fair share of situations happen in life that humbled me since I was too proud, or should I say, too busy to do so at the time.

My daughter and I had a good relationship, but I could see something was troubling her. Right before the COVID-19 pandemic exploded, she became an endangered runaway. My life felt as if I'd hit a brick wall. I was emotionally shattered. My husband and I had to declare her missing. We had always been a private family, but this situation deemed it necessary to publicly share for her well-being. Police, our community, close family, and friends diligently helped us search for her.

During this time, we were simultaneously loved and embraced by some while also shunned and judged by the very ones we least expected. This was a situation I had never prepared to experience. You know how you hear of children missing or running away, and sure you may share fliers and say a special prayer for them and their families, but it's a pain you don't quite understand until you go through it. To all the families who have walked a similar path, my heart yearns for you.

This was one of the most stressful times in our family's life. However, we prayed, believed, and trusted that God would bring her home safe and God did just that. My life went from being overwhelmingly busy to a complete halt. There was no more passing each other in the wind. I had to choose the career I wanted or the family God blessed me with. In an instance, I had to let go.

Shortly after, it would be discovered that my daughter was molested by a cousin years prior. Our goal was and always is for the health and safety of our children. Though no justice was brought to her, I know God will vindicate her. Watching her pint up with anger, hurt, and getting scared and confused, my job was to support her, be a listening ear, and get her the best help I could. This was a journey I could have never prepared myself for.

The truth was, I had also been assaulted as a young girl. My daughter's journey made me unpack the trauma and façade I had been holding on to for years. I was no stranger to pain. Though I thought I'd forgiven everyone, the anger, hurt, and resentment within me were still lingering in the shadows. Her pain triggered mine. I knew I wasn't completely healed, and I knew if I didn't release them, God could not fully work in me. So, my journey began. I was tired of feeling stuck. I needed to let it all go and release what was holding me back.

Chapter 2: Generational Curses

Lurking in the dark corner of your life is a compartmentalized area that nobody knows exists but you, God, and maybe your closest friends. This area that gets covered and sometimes forgotten pertains to generational curses. For the most part, everyone's family has its share of baggage and stories that remain untold. There are skeletons in closets, and some even go to their graves without ever uttering a word of what they've endured. Everyone has a chapter in their book of life that no one gets to read intentionally, and that secret chapter carries with it the heaviness of what has happened effortlessly.

Nonetheless, just because a problem, situation, or stronghold does not get spoken of and addressed does not mean that it did not happen, nor does it mean that it will not happen to someone else in your lineage. The enemy knows everything about you; he's been studying you, your genetic makeup, and your family history. For years, he has successfully allowed families to succumb to the same demise because there are situations that get swept under the rug, people turn their heads even when they see the wrong, or no one wants to admit that certain events are truly happening in their lives because they would much rather remain silent and oblivious than get involved.

If it just started with you, that would be one thing, but when you can pinpoint the same cycle happening in the lives of individuals in your family, that, my friend, is a generational curse. When we read or study the bible and see curses, we usually think of famine, immediate devastation, or disease. However, when you look around, the tactics of the curses over lives are usually so subtle people pass them off as character flaws. Never recognizing it for what it truly is, a generational curse. We see families that can't come together, siblings who won't speak, and parents that hate their children.

Understand these plots by the enemy did not just start with your parents or grandparents; these are tactics the enemy has used on people since the fall of Adam and Eve. Though God sent Jesus to reverse the curse, if we have not accepted him or if we have not asked him to break the chains of bondage, we will still repeat the cycles of those ahead of us. Now, what if you prayed for generational curses to be broken, and you still see that they have found their way into your life. How do you respond to that?

I am a mother of two beautiful young adults. I was blessed to have one of each, a boy and a girl. They are entirely different from each other and obviously so. One is a bit more rambunctious than the other, but they are both very outgoing and keep me laughing and on my toes. When my husband and I first married, we prayed that generational curses be broken from our lives, and by the time we started having our babies, those prayers became more fervent. We asked God to break the generational curses that we'd seen hinder individuals in our family. Though they were topics that were not discussed amongst our families, they were undoubtedly apparent, and we addressed them in our marriage.

I was personally a product of divorce, abuse, and abandonment, to name a few. As parents, our goal in life was never to put our children through what we experienced. We prayed earnestly and asked God to break the cycle and break the curse. Though nothing in life is perfect or guaranteed, we give our all to ensure we leave a legacy to them; not only a financial legacy but a spiritual legacy of knowing who and whose they are. Children will grow up and make mistakes, and if we as adults are honest with ourselves, we can be the first to admit that we are still growing and making mistakes as well. I know, I know, somebody reading this is perfect, but for those who aren't, you understand where I'm coming from.

You may be in the same boat and experience something as a child or an adult you promised never to put your children through. Or perhaps you didn't have children because of what you endured. I understand. Many times in life, we pray for things, and our prayers don't get answered in the way we envisioned. You find yourself going through a nasty divorce, your business fails, your child dies, or you find out one of your babies was abused, and you cringe in anger and ask, "HOW COULD THIS HAPPEN GOD, I PRAYED"?

Imagine my anger and disappointment when I discovered my daughter had endured the very abuse I prayed she would never face. Naturally speaking, we did everything we could to protect our children, and I simply couldn't comprehend what was happening. This was when true trust in God came to play. **When God asks us to trust him, it's not because it's going to be easy, but because it's going to be necessary.** I found myself saying that over and over. That phrase was in my spirit at the beginning of that year and had been getting me through many seasons.

Now I've heard cliché things about prayer that God answers yes, No, or Not Now. Yes, if it's his will, no, if it doesn't fit in his will, and not now, which is self-explanatory. But what happens when your prayers don't fit in the cliché of religion? If you don't have a relationship with God, you are going to be infuriated that the answer to your prayer doesn't fit in the religious mold. But if you trust God, no matter what you're going through or how bad it hurts, you will understand that God is truly working things out for your good.

We cannot do things in our own strength; we must rely on God to fix the wrongs in our lives. Where has taking matters into your own hands get you anyway? You're still angry, still won't forgive, still going in cycles in relationships because you won't let go and let God handle it his way. God wants to break the cycles and the generational curses in our lives. We have a part to play in that as well. We must fully close the door on what God has been saying to let go of.

We must be conscious of the thoughts we entertain and the pain we continually feed ourselves. If we are constantly feeding negativity and the things of this world, we are going to attract that and then wonder why we can't get out of the mess we are in. You've got to set time apart to get alone with God and let Him speak to you, encourage your heart, and minister to you through his word. He will reveal what has been broken in your family and ultimately in your life.

Generational curses run deep and may not have anything to do with anything you've ever done. It's just a ploy from the enemy to destroy you and your lineage. My daughter did not deserve what happened to her, I did not deserve what happened to me, and neither did you.

Everybody wants to grab hold of the blessing without acknowledging the generational curses that exist. God wants to deliver you from the past and free you from the downfall that has taken hold of so many in your family line. As a mother, I don't want to see my children go through what I've experienced. With God as our heavenly father, he doesn't want the cycle, the curse, the pain, the lack to continually overtake your life. God wants to overtake you with the plans and purpose that he had for you in the beginning. Will you trust him?

Chapter 3: Cleaning out the Closet, literally!

Every few years, I clean out my closet and bless others with shoes, perfume, and clothes. I noticed a few years ago that I had a lot of old things. So, I decided it was time to purge. It took some time to get it to my satisfaction. It got real on the last night of cleaning and going through things. Emotionally real.

I realized clothes and shoes didn't bother me to get rid of as much as the purses and perfumes. For some reason, they had more sentimental value to me. Perhaps because the purses had been with me so long. I used to like straw purses for the summer and found several stuffed in the back of the shelf, cracked; it was sad to see. I found completely worn leather purses. "I could've kept them as vintage pieces," I rationalized to myself.

Some items were given as gifts that I never used. Other items I had purchased with the tags are still attached. I had perfume with just a few drops left that I didn't want to part with because the smell reminded me of a particular time in my life. I could remember wearing a particular purse in high school, the first black purse my husband bought me, hand-me-down purses my "momma" gave me.

As I looked around, I thought, you'd better part with this stuff, or you're going to be on hoarders. I closed my eyes, and remembered the events surrounding a particular purchase I made, when I used a particular item, or the person who blessed me with it. (Hey, don't judge me, this was emotional.) At that moment, something miraculous happened. I let go!

I realized I had accumulated so much without letting go of anything. So, if the purse was in good condition and I hadn't used it in a year or more, it went into a blessing box. Clothes that had the tags, but I knew I wasn't going to lose or gain weight to fit into, had to go, including the shoes. I gave away barely used bottles of perfume that smelled good but no longer smelled good on me. Tossed bottles that hardly had anything left and only kept what I used often; I only wanted things that served a purpose in my life.

This may seem like a small feat to some, but it was very soothing, satisfying, and necessary. What I realized was this experience wasn't just limited to cleaning out my closet. This was about my life, as I am sure many of you reading can relate as well. I had no problem letting go of so many aspects of my life and people. However, there were things, people, and situations that I had a problem releasing.

I had to let go; it was beyond necessary. There were so many things, people, and situations that no longer served a purpose in my life, used me for convenience and dragged my name through the mud, but for some reason, I held on to them. As I got quiet and took emotional inventory, I was able to see the value of what I had and let go of what or who just took up space and energy. Every situation or person served a purpose at one time. Nothing gets wasted in our lives. Going down memory lane was emotional, but it was also soothing, satisfying, and necessary. I didn't feel the need to hold on any longer.

Chapter 4: You are Enough – Close Pandora's Box

Have you ever craved a relationship with a particular individual? Perhaps it was with an estranged family member or a distant friend? Maybe you haven't, and that's okay! But for those who have been thinking about someone, be careful what you ask for and get quiet with yourself and God to find out why you desire a particular relationship. Is it because you are lonely? Have you been trying to cultivate this type of relationship for years, and you're not a quitter, so you won't back down, even when everything around you, including your spirit, is saying to walk away? So, you keep forcing something that doesn't fit.

That was me! I grew up without my birth father but always had a desire to reconnect with him. Many times I knew it would be a bad idea to search for him, but a part of me wanted to see past what I felt. I searched for him for years, back in the day of the white and yellow pages.

When the internet started booming, I searched there too. I can't remember how often I found a man with the same name in an area I thought he lived in. I would call, only to be disappointed that it wasn't him. The person on the other line was usually gracious as I explained my search for my dad. I would take breaks for weeks at a time, and then I'd go right back to searching for him.

After over 10 years of searching, I called a number and heard the answering machine. I heard this voice I remembered so vividly as a little girl. I knew it was him. I hung up, too afraid to speak to him. I eventually called again. It was not the reunion I envisioned, nor did the relationship last. I can say, though, that I tried! There was so much I wanted to say when I had the opportunity to speak to him, but instead, I would just be happy for the moment. It was good until it wasn't. The rejection as an adult stung just as bad as it did when I was younger.

I had to let him go.

A piece of the puzzle was missing in my life and relationships. I tried to prove that I was a good child, and turned good adult, until I realized God had already approved of me. You don't have to prove your worth to people. You don't have to control or manipulate others into wanting to be with you or around you. I want to assure you that you are valuable and important. You do not need to find your worth in people.

You will never fit in when God has called you to stand out! It doesn't matter if it's a parent, a companion, or a sibling. You need to realize that you are already enough, you have been hand-picked and chosen by God, and you don't have to prove anything to anyone but yourself.

So just be careful to who you open the doors of your heart too. Everyone has a little baggage, but some people are walking around with every emotional trauma, compounded with their negativity and family, and you ask yourself, did I really sign up for this? When you enter a relationship or are born into one, it's hard not to let their problems become yours. As much time as you spent idolizing, fantasizing, or longing for this relationship, you are now franticly trying to see how you can get out on the next thing smoking.

You've just opened yourself to Pandora's Box. You wanted that new friendship, wanted that child/parent relationship or wanted to belong so bad that you opened yourself up to a host of other things that are not good for you. One of the main reasons for this is that people are usually moved by emotion and their own desires instead of waiting on God. They have placed so much emphasis on relationships, making more money, or making a name for themselves, that these things have become their highest priorities in life.

All the while, God is standing there wondering when you are going to put down the idols in your life and get back to him. He's waiting for you to seek Him above everything and watch Him provide you the best of everything. It's just not worth it to place God in second place.

News Flash: I needed to remind myself who I was outside of my career or the lack of not having my father. I had to remind myself that my value wasn't wrapped in my accomplishments. I needed to look within myself, at my marriage and my children with fresh eyes, and see that everyone was evolving, and I wanted to be a part of that picture. I had to trust that even though God allowed me to be a part of his permissive will, I wanted to be smack dab in the center of it.

I know it's easy to become focused on what's tangible or attainable, but you've got to set your expectations higher, set them on whatever is a part of God's pleasing and perfect will for your life. If something feels wrong for you, stop fighting it, stop settling for second best. I believe that God has good things in store for you, but you will not experience them until you elevate your way of thinking and be okay with walking away.

Stop allowing people to place a demand on your time and drain the energy out of you. Stop allowing others to not respect your boundaries and blame the cause of another bad friendship or failed relationship on you. Stop listening to the lies! When you are not desperate, your decision-making will be much clearer. Stop falling for the Okie Doke; please close Pandora's Box.

If you can relate and you feel stuck in a situation or with a friendship because you don't want to hurt someone, or you're the person who just won't let go, you've got to follow the peace in your heart so you can have the peace in your life. If you are a believer in God, I strongly encourage you to seek him first. He promises that when we seek him first, everything we need will be added to us. We don't have to go around trying to make things happen in our own power and strength. We don't have to go through life frustrated because of every wrong turn or choice, we can trust God.

Have you ever had a friend come to you for advice because you are knowledgeable about a plethora of things? They've talked to you for hours, and you've told them your mistakes, your victories, and how they, too, can overcome. They may have listened or may have only come to you because they wanted you to be on their side (whether they were right or wrong). Then the next month or a few months later, they are coming to you again for yet the same scenario. Eventually, you get tired of them wasting your time if they are not going to listen.

Now I am going to say something that you may not like but hear me. What good is asking God to speak to you if you never planned on listening anyway? What good is it to beg and plead and cry and waste your time (and God's) if you plan to do things your own way? I know that God's ways don't always make sense and don't always go with popular opinion, but God's ways are higher than ours, and HE protects us when we trust him.

As you read this, I pray you to remember that you shouldn't settle for less because you are valuable. You don't have to chase relationships, money, status, or titles; when you are in alignment with God, the right people will eventually be connected to you, and there will be no doubt that the restoration and good things you are experiencing are because of the hand of God.

Chapter 5: The Season of Healing and Letting Go

In my spirit, I keep hearing this is a season of healing and letting go. The weather is changing, the leaves are starting to change colors, the air is crisper, and it's time to let the leaves that are not meant to be a part of our lives fly away. This is a season of letting go, and I know it has been easy in some relationships and much harder in others.

You don't realize how much of a burden someone is to your emotional and physical health when you are constantly justifying their behavior to yourself and others. You never notice how much you have taken until you reach a breaking point, triggered by nonsensical accusations. At the same time, the true culprit of the failing relationship is not open for discussion.

"There is a time for everything, and a season for every activity under the heavens......A time to search and a time to give up, a time to keep and a time to throw away" (Ecclesiastes 3:1,6, NIV).

Some relationships can be salvaged. When growth, boundaries, honesty, and transparency are expected and given from all parties, you will see the flower of love start to blossom again.

However, when you've experienced years of rejection, years of hatred, a promise to make things better, and continual let-downs intermittently sprinkled with glimpses of hope, all to be thrown away because the stale person they were just moments earlier can't seem to fathom that God created differences on purpose. That your life is yours to be lived to the full, not to be like the other person, coveting what the other person has, angry because of every failed attempt they've had is simply because they are living in another's shadow, and too afraid to emerge and become the greatness they were created to be.

Oh yes, it's easier to point the blame to justify one's behavior, but it takes courage to look within and see the dwindled version of what you have become and speak life to that victim mentality into the Victor mentality that God wants you to dominate.

Many times, a person is too afraid to break away from the familiarity of the pain they've endured, constantly attacking the ones they claim to love in an aggressive or passive-aggressive manner. Through this, the resistance becomes easier to let go of. Letting go of anything is hard to do. So many times, we are holding on for dear life, we love hard, we promised no matter how hard it got, we would stick it out. Our hands are bruised from grabbing as tight as we can, trying not to lose that grip, trying not to escape the inevitable, but honey, the inevitable is just that. There are some relationships that you must let go of. It may not be goodbye to them forever, but in this season, in this moment of time, you've journeyed as far as you are allowed.

Sometimes God brings relationships back full circle. I am a firm believer in God's restorative power, I have even experienced restoration myself several times, but I also know that there comes a time when enough is enough. You've been lied to and lied to too many times. This person may have tried to manipulate those closest to you to think differently about you. In their rage at your continued success, they have just continued to set themselves up for failure. God is not going to bless the connived mess conceived against you.

Honest communication could circumvent so much of the distance, with the individual not knowing that you are as unsure of where God is taking you as they are. However, when you show up to discuss and revive the bit of life left in the relationship and end up having a monologue with the wall while the parties who could help to rectify change are there silent, trying to pull the plug out the wall. You cannot help but let go and let that season of your life end.

Don't let titles fool you either; family is not always who you are born into. I believe it's easier to let go of co-workers, acquaintances, and so-called friends.

Those friends as close as family, family, and church folk will make you feel like you are so interwoven with them that the very prospect of letting them go leaves you broken, fragile, and torn.

The phrase letting go seems so simple, but in the grand scheme of things, while you are in the process, or you've said to yourself, "I am done with this relationship," there is emotional baggage that is left. Sometimes you will yearn for that person, no matter how bad the relationship was. It's a familiar pain that seems better than being alone but being alone is better, in the long run, to restore your soul, restore your life, and get you back on track.

You'll cry from time to time, you'll remember fond memories, and you'll also remember the not-so-great times, but what you've got to do is move forward. You don't have time to become entrapped with someone's reality of who you should be because they themselves are afraid to be free. It's ok to tell people to love you or leave you alone. Life is not like the game of tug of war. You see, if I keep pulling you towards me, and you keep pulling away, I must eventually let go. You're much too heavy for me to keep trying to pull when it's clear our lives are journeying in different directions.

Letting go is a time of reflection, which produces healing. It is going to be important to trust God like never before as you go through this season of letting go. Don't let your heart be troubled, don't be anxious about the future and who God is going to bring in that person's place if he does at all. Have the dialogue that you need so badly with your Heavenly Father. Let him bring peace and comfort to your heart and strengthen you. Listen to his voice for direction, wisdom, and for peace.

If necessary, forgive those whom you've had to let go of. It is going to be freeing for you and who you are becoming. Don't let the anger of the past control you any longer. "Get rid of all bitterness, rage, and anger, brawling and slander, along with every form of malice. Be kind and compassionate to one another, forgiving each other, just as in Christ God forgave you" (Ephesians 4:31-32 NIV). Pray for mercy for the individuals, knowing that God extended that same mercy on you.

This is just another test of your faith. Are you able to let go? Despite the trauma you've already experienced, do you want to be free? Let go of the past and those who want to keep you there. Since this is the season of letting go, go ahead, and release your grip, relax your hands, take a deep breath then exhale. Peace is on its way to you, and I pray you to receive it, In Jesus' name.

Chapter 6: A Hardened Heart

What you may not realize is that the words Fear not or don't be afraid are invaluable in our walk with God. Whether you are just coming to Christ, or you've been traveling with him your whole life. Situations are going to present themselves to you, and at that time, you get to choose whether you will trust God or be afraid. I've learned that no matter how much you want to like everyone, or want to be liked, or how great you think you are, when you are chosen, God is going to harden the hearts of some individuals so he can show himself strong in your life. Stay humble, and your life is going to be an adventure.

When God called Moses to lead the children of Israel out of Egypt, God hardened the heart of Pharaoh and the Egyptians. No one wanted to release the slaves they had been in bondage for all those years. Who would want to get rid of their cheap but extraordinary laborers? The children of Israel were far from perfect, but God had enough of hearing his people's cries, seeing their tears, and watching their pain. So, what did he do? God utilized Moses so he could demonstrate plague after plague, sparing the Israelites from danger. The misfortune that was happening to their neighbors and those who kept them in bondage was not coming near or harming God's chosen people. Why? Because God loves to show himself strong and do the IMPOSSIBLE in our lives. He is not asking for your perfection, but he is asking for your trust and cooperation!

When Moses passed on and Joshua led the children of Israel, God's hand of protection was on them like never before. Joshua 11: 19-20 NIV states, "…...Not one city made a treaty of peace with the Israelites, who took them all in battle. For it was the Lord himself who hardened their hearts to wage war against Israel, so that he might destroy them totally, exterminating them without mercy, as the Lord had commanded Moses."

We have no idea who God has chosen to harden their hearts against us. Yes, indeed, he will let you suffer for a while. The suffering doesn't feel good. Oh, but GOD will show up. It's not until we experience church hurt, work drama, unfair supervisors, uncomfortable family relationships and friendships, molestation, manipulation, and betrayal that we wonder why is this happening? What did I do to deserve this?

Many of us were too young to even speak up about the injustices that we endured at the hands of people who should've protected us. There is going to come a day when God is going to show you his purpose through all that pain. He is going to start raising you up right in front of the very people that tried to break you down. God is going to do the impossible and show himself strong in your life. Don't be afraid as you go through the process; God is going to deliver and vindicate you.

I have experienced my fair share of asking God why. I have cried countless nights, wondering if God forgot about me and why God would allow me to go through so much hurt, so much bondage, and so much grief. I had to choose between staying in the situation and becoming bitter or allowing God to bring me out and use the situation to improve me. I had to do what I was telling you to do, Not be afraid, trust God and hold on to his word when it seemed impossible.

I am a person who hates pity. I would rather deal with something and take it to God in prayer than have people feel bad for me. Like most people, I have few people close to me who know the intricate details of my life. That is extremely intentional on my part. However, I have had years of weakness, where my life was a whirlwind of disaster. In that time of testing, God spoke to me and told me I could sink or swim. I could sink without him and die way before my time or allow him to help me swim and make it to the other side. I am no dummy; I choose to swim and still choose life.

During one of the lowest times in my life, God spoke to me through his word. He said, "Do not be afraid; you will not be put to shame. Do not fear disgrace; you will not be humiliated. You will forget the shame of your youth and remember no more the reproach of your widowhood. For a moment, I abandoned you, but with deep compassion, I will bring you back. In a surge of anger, I hid my face from you for a moment, but with everlasting kindness, I will have compassion on you, says the Lord your Redeemer" (Isaiah 54:4, 7, 8 NIV).

I encourage you, yes you, the overcomer reading this, not to be afraid. God is with you. He is going to show himself strong in your life. Don't worry yourself about who did what, who was against you, what you brought on yourself, who didn't believe you, or who didn't believe in you. God had to harden their hearts for reasons we may never understand but trust me when I say it is all a part of his plan. He is going to take that pain that you've experienced and fuel you with power, fuel you with purpose, and fuel you with greatness. Get ready for it. It's coming sooner than you think.

Chapter 7: Forgive those who've hurt you, even if you don't get an apology.

Have you ever been hurt by someone? I'm talking about real hurt, real pain. Have you ever been abused? Misused? Wronged? You bare the scar mentally and physically of the assault you had to endure, yet the person is roaming around free because no one believed your story, or worse, it could not be proven. The person could even be dead, but your resentment is still very much alive. Have you ever had your name dragged in the mud and had no reason why? Most of the time, people have their own insecurities, and so they make up lies, they hurt, they harm, and they hoard. They may die never admitting what they did to you, regardless of their actions. Please know that does not nullify your truth. But what happens when you don't get an apology?

What happens when you never get the apology, the sorry that you deserve to hear.

The person continually denies the truth because they don't want to face their own fears.

You've got to free yourself and let them go if you must.

Stop torturing yourself over a relationship with no trust.

If a person doesn't take responsibility, you still have to forgive them and set them free.

Why? Because you deserve happiness and a clear mental capacity.

Your life is worth living, and no one can ever take your place.

Your value is immeasurable, so keep journeying on this human race.

Sometimes you'll never get the closure you want, so don't let those words be the ones you long to hear. You owe it to yourself to let go of the pain, forgive them, and be free. Continue working on yourself, get up and go on with your life. Through the pain, you'll find purpose.

Many individuals are naturally predisposed to forgiving. They may get angry over their past, and rightfully so, but they choose to forgive, let go, and follow a higher path. They are not recounting every situation or allowing themselves to continually fall prey to the past. Then there are the individuals that are so angry they will go as far as to hold a grudge against an inanimate object. We've seen those people; they've stumped their toe on a chair, and now they avoid that chair at all costs. I know it sounds extreme, but it's real. The grudges that are held create such toxins in one's body that a new type of pain is created by not releasing and letting go.

When you've suffered so many injustices in life, it's easy to want revenge. It may not seem unreasonable to make others suffer the way you have, to treat others worse than the way they treated you, to build walls that you will never allow anyone to tear down. However, the entire time your mind is on the tangent of what must be done to rectify your hurt, the deepest core of you just wants peace. I must tell you there is one more thing you must do to fully embody the peace that your soul needs. That thing is forgiveness.

If you are living in shame, living in pain, and afraid to let go, you are inevitably hurting yourself. Some of you may be self-harming, cutting, biting, or choking; then there's fornication, adultery, drugs, and alcohol. These are some natural things that temporarily dull the pain. At the end of the day, I know your soul is tired and weary. It's easy to masquerade. No one can see the scars, and covering up what you don't want exposed is easy. But what happens when you encounter others? As much as you want to be free and happy, a bit of pain will ooze out and eventually overflow and ruin relationships.

I know that people may have let you down, wronged, and betrayed you. They may have promised you one thing and done the complete opposite, know that "God is not human, that he should lie, not a human being, that he should change his mind. Does he speak and then not act? Does he promise and not fulfill?" (Numbers 23:19 NIV). Many times, it's easier to trust in someone or something tangible, but the frailties of doing so can leave you wounded and broken. You've got to trust God with every fiber of your being, knowing that if he said it, if he promised you, if he spoke to your spirit, you can count on him to show up and perform. He is well able.

Hurt is real, trauma is real, rejection is real, and pain is real. Having a mother or father who didn't love you, gave you up, didn't understand you, mistreated you, and behaved in ways you would have never imagined a parent could do is unbearable. Having an uncle, cousin, or stranger physically and emotionally abuse you, and all you could do was cry and whimper, with those around telling you to "Shut Up, Stop Whining, or Nothing Happened to You." It's natural to recluse while you carry the hurt and the shame and the burden as if it were really your fault. Suffering from abandonment from the father who walked away, the ones who said they loved you. The siblings who turned their backs, the spouse that humiliated you, and the friends that were nowhere to be found when times got tough. The business deals that went sour, and not to mention the money you invested that you can never recoup.

These are the condensed but real stories that have affected the lives of so many that we encounter daily. Those who mask the pain and try to smile, but deep inside, they are hurting, they are scared, and they feel hopeless. If you can relate to any glimpse of pain as noted above, remember that you are an Overcomer, and there is no accident that you are reading this. Perhaps you have never uttered the pain that you've endured. You've suffered quietly but want nothing more than to let go.

You may feel like you've been the bull's eye in the dart game of life. Each sting of pain has left you questioning the why's of life; "Why was I born to endure this, why me, or Why Am I Even Alive"? Though one may never get the answers to life's questions that they seek, holding on to the hurt ultimately does more harm than good. When you make it over the hurdle, you'll understand your ability to help someone else, but going through the valley is a tough pill to swallow.

I don't care who you love that won't love you back, and I don't care who doesn't support you, who doesn't believe in you. I don't care who criticizes your every move. You don't have time to dwell on anything that will keep you from the prize, from reaching your goals and fulfilling your dreams. The word of God says, "Be strong and courageous. Do not be afraid or terrified because of them, for the Lord your God goes with you, he will never leave you nor forsake you." (Deuteronomy 31:6 NIV). You can't keep letting negative behaviors and comments bring you down. I know it can be difficult, I know it can be stifling, but block the naysayers, block the outside voices, block the negativity. You've got to keep going, and God will bring you the right people in His time. Until that happens, prepare your heart and mind for the things you desire. Believe me when I say there are greater days ahead.

God has not forgotten you, nor will he ever forsake you. Nothing in life gets wasted, no matter how you feel, you did not go through and endure those hardships for nothing. I know it's been hard; you've sacrificed; you've felt humiliated and rejected, but believe me, God has not forgotten you.

Prayer: Lord, I pray that you bless the overcomers that read this. Touch them in their mind, bodies, and souls. Let them give the hurt and the pain over to you. Let them embrace the fact that you love them, and you will vindicate them. Let them receive the healing that only you can provide. Lord, I also pray for mercy for those who have caused the stumbling blocks in their lives. I pray that they confess to you what they've done so you can free them from the guilt that has haunted them. Above all, I pray for healing and wholeness to flow. In Jesus' Name ~Amen

Chapter 8: Take Personal Inventory – Forgive Yourself

Have you been struggling with past mistakes? Have you committed a sin (or several sins) for which you feel God just won't forgive you? Are you carrying the burden of yesterday? If you answered yes to any of these questions, I want you to know that there is grace for you. Always remember, once you've repented, all is forgiven.

You will never be truly free if you don't forgive yourself in addition to those who have caused you pain. It is important to see forgiveness as one of the most important steps in the process of freeing yourself.

You can and should talk to a therapist, or a trusted friend, and take it to God in prayer, but forgiveness is not something you can request people to pray for on your behalf. This is a process that requires you to do the work for yourself.

My mother and I were chatting over the season of letting go and the reality of what happens when we hold on. There is so much bitterness that callouses the hearts of individuals and keeps them from fully enjoying the best life that God intended. Unforgiveness is a toxin that slowly kills you. Medical experts agree that un-forgiveness is a cause of depression, anxiety, stress, and certain diseases. Forgiveness provides a natural way to reverse some of the medical ailments you may feel.

There is always a great emphasis placed on forgiving one's offender, and I truly believe that is necessary. However, the most important person to forgive today is yourself. Forgive yourself for judging yourself harder than necessary, for not allowing your mind to forget all the trifling things you've done. Forgive yourself for not valuing YOU as God sees YOU. Forgive yourself for always trying to carry the load alone.

Today I want to challenge you to take a personal inventory of your life and its relationships. We emphasize what a person has done to us and how we've been offended, hurt, rejected, abandoned, etc. That we rarely assess how we've behaved over the months or years with those around us. We've all heard the saying "Hurt people hurt people,"; and while many justify the reasons why they hold grudges, spew hate, and general avoidance, rarely does one take inventory of themselves to say – 'Have I been the offender?'

I don't believe that anyone hurts others intentionally. You have some people out there who seek revenge and payback, but ultimately, hurt is deeply engrained and perpetually generational. No one truly seeks to hurt the ones they love, yet every person on this planet has been hurt at least one time in their life. If we are honest with ourselves, we can admit that we've caused unintentional hurt to others.

I always see it with parents and their children, spouses, and friendships. Generally, when someone is speaking about the hurt they've endured, it is usually one-sided. Granted, there are several situations where individuals are being downright abused, and there is nothing they ever did to bring about the abuse. Please understand I am not condoning abuse or justifying behaviors. What I am saying is that in relationships, one may be completely oblivious to the hurt they are causing you because they are trying to heal from their pain from long ago. Because many on this earth are hurting, they are also hurting others in the process.

It's usually not just the hard-core, obnoxious person who is malicious with their words and actions, but it's the super sweet person you may have never expected to lash out. This teaches us to never judge a book by its cover. Life has a way of bringing us full circle to an experience that haunted us, we are triggered, and the pain and memories flood us. How we respond and react is completely our choice.

Every action has a reaction, and when you think logically, you remember that every action has a consequence. Though you may have done something that you felt would've only hurt yourself, you soon realize that your actions affect others around you as well. If you have offended others by your actions, you should most definitely go to them for forgiveness. This doesn't mean they will forgive you. Sometimes people want you to hurt or see harm come towards you, depending on the magnitude of the offense. Many times, though, the punishment for one's actions isn't viewed in ways that others notice but comes in forms that hinder one's own spirit, such as unhappiness, insecurities, fear, shame, and regret.

Individuals are quick to point the finger at who's done them wrong, stolen time, money, or resources from them, and very rarely has someone judged themselves with the same measuring stick that they are using with others. Many are quick to want forgiveness and mercy from God and others but are hesitant in how they forgive others, if ever.

As believers, we don't want to go around causing stumbling blocks to others. We see individuals making a conscious effort not to hurt co-workers, church folk, and strangers, but have not been as merciful to those who are closest to them.

Today I challenge you to move beyond yourself. Take inventory of the hurt and pain that you've caused in others around you. Go to God about what you've done. Reach out to the individuals if they are willing to talk to you. If not, write a letter and state the hurt you've caused to others, repent of your wrong and then either shred or burn the letter up. This will be a physical way to let go of burdens that have held you down emotionally. I promise you it will be freeing as well.

If you have extended forgiveness to someone and they've rejected it for whatever reason, that is quite alright. You did your part. Do not try to figure out one thousand ways for them to see things your way. If you let go of the bitterness, the hurt, the shame, there is no need to pick it back up. Forgiveness does not mean that there will always be reconciliation. Of course, Jesus is our ultimate example of reconciliation and restoration, but people are still people at the end of the day. Forgiveness is a process, and people heal when they are ready.

Understand that offenses will come. Hurt people hurt people. But we don't want to cause stumbling blocks to others. If you are honest with yourself, you have done some wrong to others too. Perhaps it wasn't with the same intensity or to the same degree, but you are not as perfect as you'd like others to think. None of us are. We are all perfectly imperfect.

Pray for those who persecute you and use you. Pray especially for those who you've hurt. Pray that God heals their broken heart and that they find peace. I pray that God goes to the deepest darkest part of your soul and illuminates you with his presence. Pray for mercy and grace for them, understanding that one day you are going to need someone to extend that same mercy and grace to you. When you are done taking inventory, praying for them, and writing and burning up your letter, I want you to get up and walk with your head held high. I don't want you sulking about what could have been. You have a new opportunity to be a better you, the person God ordained in the beginning.

There may be other things that you need to forgive yourself for, so take a moment and do just that. Find that inner peace that your soul needs, that tranquility in knowing that you are okay. You've weathered many storms, you've gone through several seasons, some that should have killed you, yet you are still alive today, still standing strong. Yes, the bruises are still there; they are signs of your survival. So don't beat yourself up anymore for what you could have been or what you didn't do. Learn to enjoy this moment, this day. This is your season of forgiveness and letting go of what's been eating you up all these years. Release it in Jesus' name.

Take a deep breath, exhale, and set the butterfly of your soul free. You've been cocooned long enough. It's time for your metamorphosis to take place. First spiritual, then natural. When you forgive, you allow growth to take place on so many levels. I believe that as you start to forgive yourself for what you've done, and once you forgive others that you will start to see doors open like never before. You will still encounter storms, but you will have the propensity to let go sooner, forgive quicker and trust God as your life depends on it, because it does.

Emerge from the darkness or the dimness that has tried to trap you. Follow the path of light, the path of peace, the path that God already laid out for you. Your very own unique path. There is freedom in being authentic. Freedom in rising higher and knowing that you are loved, you are forgiven, and you are free.

Trust that many opportunities are going to arise to threaten this freedom, this new forgiven and forgiving you. Your mind and heart will be at odds over how you should treat yourself and how you should treat others. But you have something powerful backing you up, and it's found in the word of God. Allow nothing or no one to rob you from living free from worry and anxiety, and you are free from the poison.

When the enemy tries to remind you of your past, remember you've forgiven yourself, and most importantly, God has too. "For the Lord you God is gracious and compassionate. He will not turn his face from you if you return to him" (2 Chronicles 30:9, NIV). "He (God) does not treat us as our sins deserve or repay us according to our iniquities. For as high as the heavens are above the earth, so great is his love for those who fear him; as far as the east is from the west, so far has he removed our transgressions from us" (Psalm 103: 10-12 NIV).

Because we know that God forgives us and continues to love us despite ourselves, we must graciously extend that same forgiveness, love, mercy, empathy, or whatever is needed to exemplify Christ. "And when you stand praying, if you hold anything against anyone, forgive them, so that your Father in heaven may forgive you your sins" (Mark 11: 25 NIV). "For if you forgive other people when they sin against you, your heavenly Father will also forgive you. But if you do not forgive others their sins, your Father will not forgive your sins" (Matthew 6:14-15 NIV).

I challenge you to emerge during this season of letting go, this season of forgiveness, and this season of healing. Nothing is by accident, and though this journey is going to be difficult at times, it is also going to be freeing and satisfying. I know God is ready to use you. He's prepared you. It's your transformation time, so Forgive, Let Go, and Be Free. Don't worry about how people think you should behave, forgive, or live. Make up in your mind that you are going to do things God's way from here on out.

"Do not conform to the pattern of this world but be transformed by the renewing of your mind. Then you will be able to test and approve what God's will is - - his good, pleasing, and perfect will" (Romans 12:2 NIV).

Chapter 9: You are Forgiven and Restored

I know you may have struggled with shame, regret, and other hindrances, but understand God is not like people. Every time you come to him in prayer, he is not whispering and reminding you of your mistakes. People may do that, and the enemy most certainly does; but God wants to restore you and forgive you, he wants you to be whole and entire in him, lacking nothing. He does not want you defeated by sin, especially since he sent Jesus to conquer sin for us.

Once you've repented, I want you to focus on the grace of God. Grace is the unmerited and undeserved favor of God. Grace is not something we could have earned, yet God so graciously bestows his love for us by not punishing us the way we deserve to be punished by man's standards. Grace is the second, third, and fiftieth chance that God has given you simply because you've repented, and he loves you.

When you start feeling overwhelmed by your past, I want you to remember God's grace, favor, and mercy in your life. Our minds can be our strongest battlegrounds. Though you know you are forgiven and believe in God's grace, you will be tempted to think about your past, but you are forgiven and restored. This does not mean you will be perfect and never make another mistake or ever sin again, but it does mean if you are presented with the same tactics from the enemy, you can identify it and overcome it.

No one graduates to the next level academically until they pass the test required for the course. Likewise, we as believers will not graduate to the next level God wants to take us to until we are able to pass the test (which may include one that you have previously failed). Some tests will look similar, and others you may not even notice until you're right in the middle of it. Just know God has equipped you to overcome. If you fail again, please do not stay there feeling like you are a failure and that your world is going to end. You are not defined by your past or your mistakes. You are capable of more than you can imagine. You are Enough.

Know that God knows every step you are going to take and has taken every fall into account. When you feel the strongholds of the past, try to grip you, get back up, and remember God's grace, favor, and mercy in your life. Let God's words become ingrained in your heart and in your mind. You must love what God loves and hate what he hates to fully tap into and maintain a repentant heart. By the grace of God, you can do it.

Chapter 10: Love Yourself

If you are finding it difficult to look past your childhood, your adulthood, your mistakes, what happened to you, things you couldn't control, or maybe things you could've controlled but felt easier to comply with…. I want you to do something today and every day after that. I want you to tell yourself that you are loved, that you are forgiven, you are restored, you are valued, you are enough, and you are free. You are free from the guilt, free from the shame, free from the disappointment, free from trying to carry the load on your own. God wants to heal you.

So, what is the first focus: To Love Yourself! Until you love yourself, you truly can't love anybody else. Once you love yourself – loving others becomes easy. Matthew 22:36-39 NIV, "Teacher, which is the greatest commandment in the Law? Jesus replied: Love the Lord your God with all your heart and with all your soul and with all your mind. This is the first and greatest commandment. And the second is like it: Love your neighbor as yourself." Once you love yourself, the rest will follow and fall right into place.

Always remember who you are.

You are fearfully and wonderfully made.

You are the righteousness of God in Christ.

You are the head and not the tail.

You are clothed with strength and dignity.

You are secure.

You are confident.

You are amazing.

If you are finding it hard to accept these truths, I have a few scriptures for you to meditate on that will encourage you. Say these over and over to yourself, get them in your spirit, and put a note in your closest, on your phone, on your car's dashboard, on your refrigerator, or in your bathroom. Do whatever you have to do until you believe these truths about yourself.

- Psalm 139:14 NIV, "I praise you because I am fearfully and wonderfully made; your works are wonderful, I know that full well."

- 2 Corinthians 5:21 NIV, "God made him who had no sin to be sin for us so that in him we might become the righteousness of God."

- Deuteronomy 28:13 NIV, "The Lord will make you the head, not the tail. If you pay attention to the commands of the Lord your God that I give you this day and carefully follow them, you will always be at the top, never at the bottom."

- Proverbs 31:25 NIV, "She is clothed with strength and dignity, and she laughs without fear of the future."

For most of us who have endured heartache, that pain didn't occur overnight, but there was a buildup of allowing others to mistreat you, or you were afraid to speak up for yourself. Accepting what happened to you does not make it right, but it does allow you to face it head-on and heal. You deserve to be free. So, give yourself time to heal, time to recover. Be patient as you digest who God has called you to be. Let go of the anger and the resentment. It will take time, but I guarantee you – you are going to be empowered, you are going to be free, and you are going to lead others into victory.

Pretty soon, loving yourself and others are going to be as natural as breathing. Look in the mirror and tell yourself one truth. Say, "I LOVE ME" do not walk away from that mirror until you believe that you are worthy of love and to be loved. It doesn't matter if you must scream it or whisper it. Just don't walk away until you mean it. You may have to do this several times, for several minutes or hours, over the course of several days or months. Don't say this nonchalantly but with intensity and strength. I want you to remember who you are and all the happiness you deserve. It all starts with you.

Doesn't that feel good knowing that you are loved, knowing you are forgiven, and knowing you are free? Keep your freedom. Don't go back to your old way of thinking or rationalizing, you have done a 180 on that portion of your life.

53

Chapter 11: Let's Break Down the Lies

Our children can take us for a ride. Sometimes we can have fun with them, and the next minute become completely frustrated with their choices and decisions. No matter what they do, as parents, we always love them. You may need to give them tough love and let them figure out something on their own when they believe they know everything and refuse to listen, but as a parent, we've been there and done that - and most of us are providing wise counsel. When they refuse to listen, we still love them.

There is a common misconception that life becomes a breeze when a person is saved, believes in God, and has accepted Jesus as their Lord and Savior. An individual who has given their life to God is sometimes expecting all their crooked paths to be made straight, and outsiders are expecting close to perfect behaviors due to their new conversion. This is such a fallacy, and many individuals turn away, deem hypocrisy, and never question their own cynicism. Just as a child grows naturally, one must also grow in their faith walk.

It hurts me to see so many children and adults in the world, blind, confused, frustrated and torn between who they want to be and what the world wants them to be. If we are all honest with ourselves, we have either struggled or are struggling with our identity in this world. Should I be who

God wants me to be? What does God want from me? The path of sin is so flagrant yet attractive to many, and without hesitation, without notice, without a blink of an eye, we find ourselves enticed by the very things that should repel us. The very things that God has commanded us and said, "Thou shalt Not," we find ourselves saying BUT and later justifying our behaviors.

The Apostle Paul summed it up best for me. He said, "I do not understand what I do. For what I want to do I do not do, but what I hate I do. And if I do what I do not want to do, I agree that the law is good. As it is, it is no longer I who do it, but it is sin living in me......So I find this law at work. Although I want to do good, evil is right there with me." (Romans 7:15-17, 21 NIV).

If you have ever found yourself on the wrong side of the fence or on the outside looking in, know that you are not alone. I strongly believe that God loves using perfectly imperfect people. In fact, the Bible does not hide the imperfections of many of the great heroes of the Bible. They were flawed, they were broken, they were scared, and they were human. As many times as I've heard someone say when they get to heaven, they want to give Adam and Eve and others a piece of their mind, I dare to fathom our role in humanity today and how we see, hear, and read of the examples and the wrongs done millennia's ago, and yet and still make the same mistakes and cover our faults or let pride get in the way. The reality is that we share in our humanness and have similar traits and character flaws.

I will say when our children are babies, they are perfect. As they grow, they are sweet and inquisitive, and our goal is to shower them with love, affection, and admiration. As they grow into adulthood, they often forget our teachings. The world is awaiting them, and though you have trained them in the fear and admonition of the Lord, some will stray and want to find life their own way. When I grew up, children were to be seen and not heard. That was probably the dumbest way to view children. Children have feelings, they go through things and grow through things and need validation, direction, and their opinions heard, respectfully.

I always wanted to have and have had open communication with my children. I understood the pain of masking; I knew too well what holding it in did and not being believed, and so I never wanted my children to ever feel that way. I wanted them to know that I loved them, and they could tell me anything, no matter how bad or how good. God loaned my children to me, and with all I have in me, I must protect, love, and nurture them. It took me too many years to become free, so my goal was to ensure they experienced the freedom that Jesus died to give them.

This does not mean that any of us will be perfect at life, but it means that we give it our best shot every single day. No matter how great of a parent you are, you can't shelter your children from the world. You can only monitor so much. Proverbs 22:6 KJV states, "Train up a child in the way he should go: and when he is old, he will not depart from it." What does that mean for us? It means once we've deposited the word of God in their hearts and instilled virtues in them, they may stray, but they will find their way back home. One day the light bulb will come on, and they will remember the teachings, the love, the word of God, his protection, and his provision, and they will want to return. Not saying that everything is going to be perfect, but a life with Jesus is far better than a life without him.

If you have a child who's strayed, who's living their life however they want, and it goes against everything you've taught them, don't be discouraged; they will return. As hard as it is to relinquish your hold and your worries, you must give them back to God and trust HIM while you go through the process. This is not just for natural children; this is what is necessary to do with spiritual children as well. Just as God has entrusted natural children to our care, he has entrusted spiritual children to churches, ministries, communities, and groups.

Trust the mender of everything to restore his children. I strongly believe that there is going to be a great return of God's children. They will no longer be swayed by the opinions of people, no longer enticed by the carrots dangled in front of them by the world. They will want something real; they will want a relationship, fellowship, and love, and God is going to have his people who are positioned on this earth, with his heart, ready to embrace them and shower them with love. Not judging them but loving them. With the understanding that nothing they've done has separated them from God's love for them.

As a mother who has welcomed home a missing child, I know that feeling of relief, compassion, love, and grace that you give your child as you hold them tight, celebrate them, and with God's help, lead them to a road of recovery. There are so many people (children of God) who are missing in action, lost, and hurting, but one day, and I believe one day soon, they are going to come to themselves, and they will return home.

God is already there, waiting with open arms. He wants his body of believers to be on the same page, ready to embrace them and offer love, grace, and compassion. We are the representation on earth as it is in Heaven. We must be about Kingdom business. Our Heavenly Father is waiting for you to return home. He's not mad at you, he may not like all the choices you made, but at the end of the day, he still loves you. He will never stop loving you. It's time for you to come home.

Chapter 12: Let Go of Procrastination

Lord, why do I procrastinate on the big things you've told me. When I was overworked, I blamed it on my job. I simply didn't have enough time. When I found more time, I blamed it on being tired and needing and wanting rest. When I was rested, I binge-watched Netflix movies. Most times I really enjoyed the show. There were times I would search for the creator of the show and would say to myself, instead of binge-watching, I should be creating.

By that time, I was either tired or it was time to go to work. It felt like I was in a perpetual cycle of procrastinating and not on everything, just some things. I remembered one day thinking I wanted to die empty. I do not want to leave this earth with gifts inside of me. I want to empty myself of everything God has shown me.

I prayed, Lord, let me not blame the gifts you've given to sustain me as the crutch that keeps me from fulfilling my destiny and purpose.

On another level, there is my home life and my family, and some days can be either stressful and/or busy.

Some days there is barely enough time to comb my hair (hence my hair is braided frequently or pulled back in a slick ponytail). By the time I cook, clean, play therapist, help with homework, provide a listening ear, encourage and keep others from jumping off of the proverbial bridge of life, I say okay, I'm going to now work on what I believe God has given me or dig deep into the word, but then I find myself remembering that thing called time, and usually by this time I am completely worn out.

It's a wonder I make it to the bed cause some days and nights, the sofa seems so satisfying; until I realize it's almost time to wake up and do this all over again. Prayer…. trying to incorporate time with God at the start of the day, throughout the day, and at the end of the day. Trying to build my home and have it ALL had a cost, hence the need to let go.

The truth was I wanted to build what God put in my heart and blessed me with. The career was what I wanted but not the thing deep in my heart I knew I should be doing at that time. It kept me so busy I couldn't focus on my true call. Now all the other things I was doing weren't evil things or bad things; they just overextended me from what was most important. No job, no career, no person, should become your life unless that is the life you desired. That was not my desire to let work consume me.

We hear of the Proverbs 31 woman and how she worked, got up early, and cared for her home. She built her home with love, faith, and compassion, she instilled values into her children, she respected her husband, and in return, he loved and trusted her. She was admired by those around her.

Ladies, we can be that woman today. We can have it all when we let go of the spirit of doing too much and the spirit of procrastination.

I encourage you to pray and seek God on what ***Having it All*** encompasses for you. We are accountable for our lives, our homes, and our children. This is our lot to manage as good stewards on this earth. It doesn't mean we will be perfect at it, but with intention, discipline, integrity, and a humble spirit, we can get it done.

Proverbs 31:27-28 NIV states, "She watches over the ways of her household and does not eat the bread of idleness. Her children rise up and call her blessed; her husband also, and he praises her. "

It is foolish for us to overextend ourselves and not prioritize the very life we've prayed for. It takes wisdom to humble ourselves when we seem off course and to even recognize that we are not aligned with our greater purpose.

There are so many ways that both men and women can use wisdom to build their homes. It doesn't matter how far off track you are; you can always turn and start over or pick up where you are and do better. I get it, and God knows what's on your plate.

He doesn't want you to do it alone.

He still wants you, he still wants to speak to you, and he still wants to use you. Tired and all, God will provide strength. Start small; carve at least 15 minutes a day to start working on what God has placed on your heart. It's better to start small than not at all.

Chapter 13: Moving Past Fear

What I've realized in my life and in the lives of others is that procrastination is just an umbrella covering the root problem. What lies underneath the umbrella could be fear. Fear that you didn't hear God right. Maybe the last time you heard God and stepped out in faith, you failed, or worse, looked like a fool.

It could be performance anxiety. Still masquerading as the fear that you won't be as good as the next person, fear that reminds you of your past and says you are not equipped to handle what you've dreamed and conceived in your heart. Fear that your idea won't take off, that you aren't talented enough. This fear keeps imprisoning you and keeps crushing your dreams.

What lies have others told you that you've accepted as truth? Have these lies become fears?

Fear debilitates. It keeps you from fully stepping out in faith. Let me remind you of this truth: God would not have given you the dream or idea without knowing you were the right person for the job. Your job is to trust and believe and step out in faith even when you feel afraid.

Hanging with the wrong crowd to fit in, allowing people to stay in your life when God told you to kiss them goodbye can stagnate your journey. Many times, we are waiting for God to move people out of our lives, and he is waiting for us to stop entertaining them. Everyone is going to experience fear over something at some time. Insecurities about our past or our appearance may come up, but you cannot let anything, not even you, stop you from persevering and fighting beyond what you think or feel. Stay focused, stay determined, because you can do this!

Don't let your insecurities get the best of you. You may have been rejected or talked down to for so long that you secretly start believing the lies. Here's the truth: You are enough. God has equipped you for such a time as this. Don't believe the lies from the devil.

Let go of the mental anguish. "For God did not give us a spirit of timidity or cowardice or fear, but (He has given us a spirit) of power and of love and of sound judgment and personal discipline (abilities that result in a calm, well-balanced mind and self-control)" 2 Timothy 1:7 Amplified Bible.

Chapter 14: Let Go of the Spirit of Perfection

How can you let go of the spirit of perfection? Give yourself grace, be vulnerable, exhale, release and give it to God. Our society has convinced us that every picture must be perfect. If not, there's a filter for that. We hide behind our flaws yet blast others for their shortcomings.

When you are alone and really take time to process your life, are you sad, unhappy, or angry? It can be as bad as when you pray and want to have intimate communication with God that you fake in his presence. You can pray like you have it all together, or you can lay out your hurts, pains, and burdens and go to God in desperation.

The same spirit comes over individuals in therapy and counseling sessions. There can be a fear of exposing too much. You will never heal from what you don't reveal. If you've grown up in a religious background or with harsh criticism, it can be hard to admit to your true feelings. Your past may have been full of fear of judgment and ridicule. However, it's ok to be flawed, fragile, and broken. No one, but God, is 100% perfect.

Don't stay in that broken state, though. Don't search for acceptance, to be liked, or to be viewed in a certain light. Let that perfection of what you want others to think about you go. Embrace the uniqueness of who God created you to be.

Chapter 15: Let Go of the Opinions of People

This is going to be an easy one for some and a hard one for many. As babies, we start learning that we depend on others for love, support, and encouragement. When we learn to walk, there's someone there to cheer us on. Somewhere along the way, those cheerleaders, parents, or caregivers disappoint. Before you know it, you've been met with an onslaught of individuals who truly don't have your best interest at heart.

Teachers, counselors, pastors, therapists. No matter the title, people are people and can and will disappoint you. If you've been surrounded by people who have only looked out for your best interest; yay for you. For those of you who've been rejected and abandoned by the very individuals who promised to be there and support you, I know the hurt is real, and it is time to heal.

Children usually want their parents to be happy with their performance in life. They will look for creative ways to gain their approval and attention, whether their performance is good or bad – they crave that attention.

They learn to look for attention, affection, and acceptance from others. Friends, gangs, romantic relationships, and supervisors, seeking approval and validation from others whether the relationship is good or bad.

I understand that everyone wants to have someone supportive in their corner. But the opinions of those around you should not dictate your worth and who you are as an individual. Whatever is said to you, process what you need and throw out what you don't.

There was an old saying, "Sticks and stones may break my bones, but words will never hurt me!" That is the biggest lie in history. Emotional abuse is exactly that…Emotional Abuse! Mental scars linger long after the physical scars heal. You may be used to individuals who verbally abuse you and have perpetuated this cycle of having individuals in your life who always find fault and tell you what you can't do or be. It's time to let go of them. To every person who wished death, failure, and disappointment on you, it's time to let them go.

Every word they've ever spoken to you may be reverberating in your mind right now. You may experience feelings of anger, resentment, or anxiety. Those are all normal feelings. When you start to process what they've said and done to you, you can be around them without feelings of animosity. You can be genuine around them, and you can shine like the light God intended you to be, whether you are acknowledged or not.

Chapter 16: Let Go of People Pleasing

Let go of people pleasing.

You are not God. I know you know that. But how many times have you played God in someone's life? When they call, you jump?! When they say they are struggling, you may take it upon yourself to fix them, give them money, a car, a place to live, food, or whatever means you have.

I've found that many times individuals will neglect what they are truly supposed to do because they are trying to fix and please the people around them. Even neglecting those within their own household because so and so needs me.

People pleasing may make you feel good for a few moments until the person starts depending on you as they should depend on God. If you feel bad, wondering if they won't like you, or if you can't help, if they will be unhappy with you; you my friend are in a cycle of people pleasing. Get off the wheel, say no, not today, not right now, but do what you need to do to end the cycle of constantly pleasing others.

You will probably feel sad, or like you are disappointing people in the beginning because it may be in your nature to want to save and help people. It is not your job to do so. Not for every call and not for every person. Many times, the people aren't appreciative. They may take you for granted or get upset when you no longer serve them as they've come to expect.

Sometimes their need and desire to need you is fear driven. They want to feel needed or waited on by you. Your value is not determined by how thin you can bend before you break. If you are in a mutual relationship of giving and taking, that is one thing. But it shouldn't always be you in a position of giving or doing everything to keep a relationship or friendship floating. Do not neglect God's call to be at the beck and call of others.

People pleasing usually accompanies guilt. You were not designed to carry the loads for others. You cannot please everyone. You may have convinced yourself that you are superman or wonder woman but don't die trying to save others and forget to save yourself in the process.

NO! You are not a pushover and do not have to agree to things to make others happy. Nor do you have to take that phone call the moment the phone rings. If you are in the space of solitude, ensure you honor your appointment to yourself, whether that be time away from your spouse, your children, your job, your extended family, and friends. So, when you reconnect with them, minutes, hours, or days later, depending on the relationship, you can offer the best version of you to everyone.

Don't feel guilty about reading that book a little longer, taking a walk alone, praying or meditating, and for those who have young children, using the bathroom with the door closed to give yourself two minutes alone. Allow yourself the space to disconnect from others and reconnect with yourself, if only for moments at a time.

Unless someone is not good for you, and only you will know that. How? The way your body responds, anxiety, for instance. Or if you just have a knowing that you can't put your finger on or unction from God. Follow that lead. Remember, God created us for relationships. Not just with him but with others as well. So, if you are strictly focused on yourself, you'll become closed and narrow-minded about what others are going through. You may also miss a window of opportunity to do good, and to speak words of encouragement, ultimately sowing a seed.

I know you've heard that misery loves company. So many times, negative individuals or gossipers breed together. It doesn't matter what city, state, or nationality. If there is a ringleader of manipulation, you can guarantee there will be some cronies. Don't fall for the trap. You were designed to go higher, to soar, and as you do, you will find individuals who are caring, supportive, and not only concerned about themselves.

No one is perfect; everyone has something that they are working towards. There are some individuals who may say I've been this way forever and refuse to change, equally wanting to keep others in that same space. The goal is to move beyond who you were and become all of what you've dreamed of and what God has promised in your spirit. That can only happen when you embrace wholeness and healthy boundaries.

Is there something in your past or childhood that made you feel like you had to please everyone?

What made you feel undervalued?

Freedom is not only found in the liberty of oneself.

Freedom is the ability to love someone and let them go at the same time.

Realizing they feel bound to you, imprisoned, stifled.

You see the energy and passion they have with everyone but you.

Don't be hurt, don't cry, and don't continually wonder, worry, or apologize.

Find your voice even in the frustrating silence of not being heard.

Set them Free. In doing so, you will free yourself.

Chapter 17: Let Go of the Need to be Accepted

Let go of the need to be accepted. God will never allow you to fit in when he has called you to stand out. You don't have to keep trying to fit in or be accepted.

I don't care if it's at church, with your family, at work, or with a group of friends. Stop telling people that you can help, I can support you, I'm on my way, when you really can't help but are merely afraid to face rejection. Many times, God will show you who to walk away from and who to leave alone, and he will reveal situations that expose who is not good for you.

If you've ever been abandoned or left alone, you generally don't want others to be in that boat. A peaceful life is about balance, not extremes.

Sometimes you may hold on to jobs, family members, churches, friends, and relationships to prove your loyalty.

Ignoring the signs that you have outgrown the situation. You may not be appreciated, you may be underpaid, but you stay to prove that you are dependable and won't let others down.

Meanwhile, you are bypassing doors of opportunity, and growth for a situation that has already let you down, abandoned you, or embarrassed and berated you.

Fear of rejection from people will keep you from obeying God, continually leaving you hurt and broken. This reminds me of giving God a "Yes" to his will but with conditions. For instance, you may tell God, "If you give me the life I want, the car, the house, the family by a certain age, I'll say yes. But when you see your plans are not being honored, you try and make it happen on your own. Even if that means going back to the people who rejected, disrespected, and undervalued you.

Yes, they may be able to help you attain some of the things but with strings attached. Strings that form more emotions of guilt, shame, and regret. You can't always see that right away because of the need to be accepted, to show others you've succeeded in an area, or to keep up with peers. God is sitting there like, "Are you done yet, Are you ready for my will for your life."

Chapter 18: Let Go of the Comparisons

If you've ever watched or participated in track and field, you'll understand the concept of running and not looking back. In a relay race, the runners don't look back but extend their hand back to pass the baton to the person behind them. They are confident, they are disciplined, and they are strategic about winning the race. Now briefly imagine your life as that of a trained runner, running a long distance, whether that be through running track, in a marathon, or a person in the Olympics. (If you aren't a runner, don't let this conversation make you feel tired, we are imagining it in a positive light right now).

Now, imagine yourself being in the lead. You can hear the cheers of the spectators all around. You don't see others around you, so you turn back to sniff out the competition. However, when you look over your shoulder, you see that people are gaining momentum and are on your heels. Now instead of focusing on winning and the finish line, you are focused on the possibility that you may not win. Your confidence is shaken, and you are discouraged. Just a few moments prior, success and the prize were in your eyes. Now you have allowed defeat to come into your heart. Why? Because you chose to look back. In the beginning, you were running the race filled with great expectations that you would go home with the prize, the gold, or the trophy; now, you are running with the fear of losing. That subtle turn over your shoulder quickly and negatively shifted the focus of your mind. Don't let that be you (anymore)!

You see, our lives can be compared to that of a runner. Understand that your mind plays a huge role in this race of life. You can only move forward by moving ahead. Sure, this sounds like a no-brainer, but you'd be surprised how many people are trying to move ahead in life but are constantly looking back. Constantly remembering the rejection, the loss, and the pain.

Looking back can be both dangerous and devastating to your future. It leaves you feeling stuck when you are always remembering what happened way back when. Just like you can be stuck thinking about what's caused you pain, you can also be stuck remembering your past victories and the good old days. "Don't always be asking, "Where are the good old days? Wise folks don't ask questions like that" (Ecclesiastes 7:10 The Message).

It's nice and, in fact, healthy to reminisce for a bit. But there is a difference between reminiscing and rumination. You don't want to allow your mind to replay every scene, re-talk every conversation in the mirror or in your head, and reexamine how you could have changed that ONE THING. Looking back doesn't always consist of bad thoughts but could consist of comparisons of who or what you had then versus where you are now. This is an awful cycle because yesterday is done, and you cannot go back and change anything. The word of God says, "Forget about what's happened; don't keep going over old history. Be alert, be present. I'm about to do something brand-new. It's bursting out! Don't you see it?" (Isaiah 43:18 The Message).

Aside from looking back at your past, looking at others can also be devastating to your future. It does no good for you to look at what others are doing or even try to keep up with those who have seemingly similar paths. I want to encourage you to allow your mind to be free, free to think about the good things that lie ahead for you. The goal is to run your own race. This is not a competition, so if you are focused on what someone behind you is doing, it is going to throw you off track and ultimately off your goal.

By understanding the mindset of the runner, you understand that looking back or over your shoulder keeps you fixated on who the runner is behind you. Stay focused, make it to the finish line, and celebrate a goal and a job well done. Do not look to see how close someone is. Are they on your heels with their vision, or are they doing the same thing, or are they going to beat you? You must keep looking forward and focused on your assignment.

How can you move on from this vicious cycle? I'm glad you asked.

First, you must identify what scares you about your past and then let it go.

Next, you must take control of your thoughts. When your mind tries to take you back to a bad time or experience, catch those thoughts and change your narrative on the situation. No longer allowing your thoughts to hold you captive to the past to become a stronghold and a stumbling block in your life.

Lastly, stop comparing your life with others. Everyone's race is going to be significantly different. Because our time spent on this earth will vary greatly from one person to the next, it's super important to ensure that you are following the plan and purpose God placed in your heart. Don't get sidetracked by whose doing what, and stop looking over your shoulder.

I challenge you to run your race. Don't look back. Don't look over your shoulder. Keep looking forward, keep your focus on winning, and do what you set out in your heart to do. Remember, what God has orchestrated for you is for YOU.

"I'm not saying that I have this all together, that I have it made. But I am well on my way, reaching out for Christ, who has so wondrously reached out for me. Friends, don't get me wrong: By no means do I count myself an expert in all of this, but I've got my eye on the goal, where God is beckoning us onward – to Jesus. I'm off and running, and I'm not turning back. So, let's keep focused on that goal, those of us who want everything God has for us. If any of you have something else in mind, something less than total commitment, God will clear your blurred vision – you'll see it yet! Now that we're on the right track let's stay on it" (Philippians 3:14-16 The Message).

Chapter 19: Let Go of Overthinking

The old version of you is always fighting for attention. There is no quick fix for your life; you have real problems, real challenges, and real decisions that you need to make. Nevertheless, let me remind you that you are here for a reason…... DO NOT get sidetracked. Do NOT give up. Do NOT allow the old version of yourself to keep you from becoming all of who you want to be and all of who you CAN be.

It's going to be a challenge, though, because our brain is filled with all sorts of thoughts, trauma, and triggers. But, if you dig deep and for some, I mean dig really deep, you'll find some happier moments and some happier times. Glean from those moments and let your mind feast on the good things instead of allowing the disappointments to rob you of a wonderful life.

There's also this glorious temple we live in that makes us feel things that aren't necessarily true. Between our flesh and our mind, we can often be deceived. Our feelings can talk us out of the very thing that we want to do, and perhaps the very assignment God put us on this earth to perform. So, what is one of the biggest culprits here? Well, I'm glad you asked. That answer would have to be overthinking.

Overthinking can keep you from taking on new goals, new tasks, new relationships, new friendships, and the list could go on and on. Overthinking has so many variants and could stem from issues such as low self-esteem, anxiety, depression, reliving past experiences, and expecting new experiences to take on the same shape and behaviors. The list can be daunting, so I will refrain from diving too deep here. Overthinking can rob you of great opportunities. By the time you debate something in your head a million and a half times, the door could be closing on something that you really wanted. Philippians 4:6 states, "Do not be anxious about anything, but in every situation, by prayer and petition with thanksgiving, present your requests to God."

When God starts speaking to your spirit and says I want you to do this or that now, or wait on this or that, be ready to follow the still small voice inside of you. Your mind and your flesh will be your biggest critics during this transitional period. They will remind you of who did what, what you didn't accomplish, what you are stronger in —weaker at -and so forth. When you start hearing all of that outside chatter trying to threaten your soul and your destiny, I want you to challenge those voices that say otherwise. Usually, when you hear something in your head that is contrary to the life you want, it causes you to overthink, rationalize, and justify.

Know that you've come too far in your life, you've been through too much, and it's time to come up higher. You may have or may never be challenged with this, but for those who have, you need to get to the root. I've had some important decisions to make this year, just as you have. I generally can reach a decision timely and keep moving forward, but I kept over analyzing this situation. It was nothing immoral or nothing that would hurt anyone, just something I was convinced for a while that I didn't need to do. When I heard this negative banter going on in my head, I asked myself out loud what the source of this negativity was. Where was it coming from? Was it from pain, fear, or an unpleasant experience, and then I immediately dealt with it! I had to meditate on the scripture, "Be anxious for nothing." This overthinking process did not last too long, but it was annoying because I knew what God said, and my flesh wanted to wrestle with my decision to trust God with the outcome.

This fight between spirit, mind, and body usually happens when God is trying to speak to our spirits, but our flesh is speaking louder. Like don't listen to that, remember when? "For the flesh desires what is contrary to the Spirit, and the Spirit what is contrary to the flesh" (Galatians 5:17 NIV). You must let go of preconceived ideas to fully embrace your goals. You can't allow your flesh or your mind to have dominion over you. So, if that means forgiving someone, letting someone go, taking on that new opportunity, just do it. Tell your past and any negative thoughts that it no longer has the authority to rob you. You are taking the authority back over your life, your situations, your circumstances, your thought patterns, your goals, your dreams, your relationships, and your career (insert anything else you need to take authority of).

Something miraculous is going to take place this year, and that something starts within you. I want you to have one of the most awesome gifts you can give yourself. That gift is peace. The peace that passes all understanding. So, when things go well in your life, and you are crushing your goals, I want you to have peace. When things are not going as expected, I want you to have peace. I don't want you overthinking and wondering a thousand what-ifs for something that may be out of your control or, worse yet, doesn't even concern you or may not ever happen.

Free yourself from overthinking. Let the old fade into oblivion. Understand how powerful and strong your mind is and train your mind to think good thoughts on purpose. Restructure the ideas that have been planted by past circumstances and build something stronger. See yourself walking into the life you've always desired. Dream again, smile again, laugh again, and not that fake stuff when you think people are watching, but be real and genuine. If you need help and a shoulder to cry on, reach out to someone. Don't be afraid to be vulnerable with those you trust. In the end, be thankful for every opportunity, for every open door,

and for every closed door. There's going to be light at the
end of the tunnel.

Chapter 20: Let go of trying to be Right

You may have been silenced for so long that you will never allow anyone to shut you up again.

Sometimes we've become so adamant about having our voices heard and ensuring our opinion gets out there to prove a point (whether bad or good). That we will engage in battles not conducive to our destinies. Have you needed to prove a point so bad that you didn't listen to the other side of the story? Trying to be right will cause you to forfeit relationships and lose opportunities.

When your only goal is to prove that you are right, it comes at the cost of ensuring that someone else is wrong.

Of course, there will be times that you need your voice to be heard, but it should not be for every frivolous matter.

Some battles in life are not worth fighting. However, when you've been backed against the wall most of your life, when you've been told "NO" or overlooked, it is probable that at every opportunity, you will take the extreme in letting others know your stance on life, work, family, even situations that don't concern you.

Before we go further, I want you to know that your voice has value. Every experience in your life matters. You are no longer that scared little girl or boy who cannot defend themselves. You are stronger now. You are wiser. You have grown. I know life has knocked you down more times than you would care to share with others.

I know you've held pains so deep in your heart that you vowed you would never be treated less than again.

What I want you to do right now is take a deep breath. Inhale. Exhale. Let it go.

Many times, peace is better than being right. Imagine if you always second-guessed your friends, your spouse, or your children.

Yes, it may have been done to you, but do you want to be bitter, or do you want to be better? Do you want everyone in your present and future to pay for the mistakes of those in your past?

Ask yourself -

Who or what situation made you feel like you had no value?

Has the need to constantly be right pushed others away? Who?

How are those relationships now?

Do you want to be right, or do you want peace?

Pain and hurt have a way of throwing you off balance. You may overcompensate by overspending, overindulging, overtalking, or overreacting. Whatever you were restricted from doing due to a state of bondage will cause you to overdo that thing when in fact, you are off balance. God wants you to have order in every area of your life.

Chapter 21: Let go of Self Doubt

We all have a dream, a vision, and a glimpse of what we believe our future should look like for ourselves and our families. We set out determined to embark on the journey and are headstrong that nothing nor anyone can keep us from reaching our goals and fulfilling the plan that we've set in motion. When we are sleeping, we can dream it so vividly that we can see it and touch it. As we are awake, we daydream about it, some of it feels far-fetched, but we trust that supernatural occurrences await us.

Let me remind you that You can do it!! You are strong enough. You have been chosen by the creator for such a time as this. Don't talk yourself out of the good life that God created for you.

Let go of the self-sabotaging thoughts.

Hold your head up high and face the enemy of doubt in your life.

If you build it, they will come

If you write it, they will read

If you make it, they will buy

You are worthy of all the good things this life has to offer.

Don't talk yourself out of it anymore.

Chapter 22: Forks in the Road

As we journey in life, we don't always realize what path to take, who should be on the journey with us, and for how long. Though we should be seeking the Lord for his guidance and peace, we get busy. We feel like it's our life, and we know what's best. Somewhere along our journey, we get to a fork in the road.

I live in the desert, and I love it. I love mountains, I love nature, and I like to hike. Every now and then, I will reach an area either walking or driving, and there will be a road sign that says dead end. You can either turn around, go left, or go right. Usually, I have a destination in mind, I can see where I want and need to be, but the sign is telling me I can't get there the way I expected to. There have been times when there was no sign, and the road ends, but common sense tells me the trail stops, and I need to find an alternate route to get me where I'm trying to go.

When we are driving, 9 times out of 10, a detour sign has been posted, and you either follow the detour path or go your own route to reach your destination. However, when we are talking about goals, dreams, and destiny, detours take on various forms that have no construction workers or road signs to keep you on the right track.

Our spiritual lives are the same way. God will show us the top of that mountain in a dream or vision, and we start journeying, happy and excited about the path that we are on. Trusting God, listening for his voice, or simply standing on what he said. However, on the way to our destination, we meet many people and start listening to other voices. Some of them we could easily do without, but then there are some that we instantly become bonded to. We love the company of certain people and sometimes ignore the red flags that surround them; because of how much we enjoy their companionship. Deep in your spirit, you know that a particular person, friendship, or habit is no longer good or healthy for you. They (it) served its purpose and allowed you to get through some fun and tough times because of God's permissive will, but God wants you to move from his permissive will into his perfect will.

Yep, you got it. The wrong kind of people can detour your destiny. Some people are like magnets for others, they attract the good, the bad, the happy, and the sad. The depressed, the oppressed, the successful, and those striving to make a good life happen. Needy, demanding, and manipulative people are lurking as roadblocks to dreams and visions. Some are inconsiderate of your time and just want to talk, generally about nothing. They lack focus and determination, and the next thing you know, you have spent hours or more with them, and your entire day/schedule is off.

Do NOT let people keep you from being determined, consistent, and focused. Please be available for emergency situations. Please set time out daily and weekly to cultivate and keep strong relationships and friendships. But do distance yourself from clingy people; they are a huge deterrent. Some people will demand time that you can't afford to always give and will suck the life out of you. Be diligent even in your friendships, realizing you are only going to be as strong as the people you surround yourself with.

Understand that the enemy will try to use individuals from your past to remind you of how much fun you used to have when you lived lawlessly; they may not like the new, mature you. They may even try to hinder you by reminding you of your past.

One of the best ways to be freed from the past is to not regurgitate what was. It's a new day. God may have even told some of you not to enter in or to stop entertaining certain friendships, but you find yourself trying to find the good when God is trying to protect you. If that resonates with you, please let it go, and follow the voice of the Holy Spirit. Know that God sees the end from the beginning and knows who and what aligns with your life.

God wants to take you higher; he wants to take you to the mountain top. There is a detour straight ahead, and if you keep going with that individual or with that habit or bad way of thinking, you will never reach what God has for you. Now your friends, habits, and thoughts will tell you that "You are tripping. You can still get where you need to go in life with me; don't let me go!" But the voice of God is going to resonate in your spirit and show you that you can only journey so far in life. You will not reach your God-given destiny and purpose if you can't let go. God has a plan to prosper you. He wants you to live an abundant life, filled with joy, a life filled with overflow. Don't let the enemy steal that from you.

To live the life you desire, you must heed the voice of God, heed the confirmation in your spirit. Understand that just because you can't see it, there is danger up ahead. Haven't you experienced enough heartache in your life? You must be willing to cut off people or things that are stagnating in your life and are keeping you from your purpose. Naturally, there may be something you are involved in that constantly brings you pain and shame, which could be a no-brainer to let go of. But what about when you are having fun with a person or situation? Yep, that makes it harder.

Some of the things that bring us pain are not easy to let go of because of being comfortable in that pain. Let me tell you; you don't have the option to stay comfortable any longer. Don't let your flesh, fun, fears, and insecurities keep you from receiving God's best. I know that my saying to let go is not going to be easy, it is going to be hard and require a sacrifice of giving up "that thing." But I promise you, letting go is going to be necessary for you to become who God called you to be and to take you from a life that is spiritually dying to a life that is full of abundance.

There may be times when you are able to journey with people forever, and you are allowed lasting and fulfilling relationships. There are also times when you come to that fork in the road with someone, a relationship, a job, a church, a business partner. DO NOT try to journey with that individual any longer, nor try to persuade them to journey with you. Once you get to that fork in the road, you will be going in two entirely different directions in life, and your paths may never cross again. You must let go if you desire to tread the path of greatness and fulfill the destiny God has for your life. Let them go at the fork in the road.

Anything worth having is worth fighting for. To become the person you've envisioned, to put the past behind you and walk into your future, you cannot stay tired, and you cannot give up. There are going to be times when your spirit is heavy, when you feel alone and when you've felt like you've done all you can do. I know it gets hard but let me encourage you to keep going. As you journey through the day, weeks, months, and years ahead, I want you to remember who you are.

God promised in his word that he would never leave you nor forsake you. He promised if He is for you, he is more than the world against you. No matter how you may be feeling, trust the creator that he is going to complete the work and the vision that he has promised for your life. Aren't you worth fighting for?

Chapter 23: Separation before Elevation

Separation always comes before Elevation. Separation rarely feels good, but it is utterly necessary to get to the next level. Journey with me......

Late in 2007 - I gave a message that's been reverberating in my spirit for the last several months. The title of the message was "I'm Prepared to Be Elevated- I've been Separated to be Transformed." What you've been going through has been annoying, frustrating, and tiring at times, to say the least. You've been experiencing a spiritual PEST. A pest is usually considered an insect or an annoying person, but while I was praying about this years ago, I perceived a pest to be something that had much more significance.

For us to be what God requires of us, it is sometimes going to feel unpleasant and downright annoying. When you feel it doesn't take all that, when you feel you can't change or when you've been struggling with the same battles- it's a nuisance, its' aggravating, and it's annoying. But a pest can be a good thing. I describe it as **Preparation, Elevation, Separation, and Transformation.**

Let's dive into the first natural and then spiritual:

Preparation = is being made ready beforehand readiness.

Elevation = to go higher. To go from a lower position to a higher rank

Separation = to set and keep apart. To distinguish and to isolate.

Transformation = a marked change for the better, in appearance, form, and nature, to be converted.

First Natural - Our lives can be described as that of a caterpillar; we start out small and wormy, and we don't stick to much of anything. We drift and slide when our mind changes. But then preparation comes. You know you have the assignment to be transformed but may not be entirely sure how the process works. The next step is elevation. The caterpillar starts looking for higher ground or a way to camouflage itself. During preparation, the caterpillar, like humans, is vulnerable, and predators see prey, but the caterpillar blends so he's not stepped on or injured by other animals. The caterpillars' goal is survival to one day transform into beauty.

Like that of a butterfly, you will transform - The next step is separation. I like you, but I can't hang with you anymore. I've got to go higher. I must be all God wants me to be. The caterpillar or pupa must spin its cocoon and is alone in insolation in the waiting process. It's separate from its kind and on its way to finishing its purpose. So, when you see me again, I won't be that slimy caterpillar, but instead, a transformation will have occurred. I will have reached my destiny, but before I fly away, I must emerge. A butterfly's body must harden to the elements, and it must be brave to fight the weather and aware of its predators. It will fly away and start a new job assisting in beautifying the world. Are you ready for your transformation to take place?

I know it's Painful, but if you don't PUSH what's in, you can't come out! We can always go back to childbirth and pregnancy. Pushing must occur. The PEST is alive and well. In our mother's womb, we were prepared and equipped with every function we would need for this world. A mother's job is like that of a church that God's assigned you to or like that of a cocoon. You are being incubated, shielded, loved, and encouraged so you can grow. But when it's separation time, everybody is aware. What's in you has got to come out. You must separate yourself and come out from among them. There's no rationalizing, no analyzing; God designed you to work together and push. The preparation is for a season; it's been agonizing, it's a nuisance, but you've got to keep going to go higher.

The elevation is different and comes in different forms. It's not about being in the public's eye or on social media. People, whether they acknowledge you or not, are watching you; some are praying for you to succeed, and some are praying that you'll stumble and fall. However, elevation is looking at yourself and seeing you are better than you were the day before. You are not where they saw you fall – last week, last month, last year. You are learning, studying, and obeying the call of God. Others will hold yesterday over your head, but the word of God says, "My mercies are new every morning, Great is thy Faithfulness" (Lamentations 3:22-23, KJV).

Then Spiritual - Elevation for birth comes different, you don't go high, but you go low; you must go down before you can come out. How many times have you noticed things seem to get worse before they get better? That's a part of natural elevation to go down then come out. In the book of Exodus, the children of Israel were delivered from Pharaoh and the Egyptians, but the children of Israel had to go down through the wilderness before they could enter the Promised Land.

The separation doesn't feel good; we like to be sheltered and want to feel supported. You may feel lonely, pain, and discouragement, but God has not left you, he's on the sideline watching you do what he has ordained for you to do. Watching you do the survival techniques, he's prepared for you. Watching to see if you're going to pass the test or wander in the wilderness. Now is the Time to start breathing on your own, start moving in the Holy Spirit, and start doing what you've been instructed to do to reach your destiny. Ready or not, you must transform- a metamorphosis is taking place.

In 2nd Kings Chapter 2, you can read how Elisha had prepared with Elijah and was bound to him. Even when he knew Elijah was leaving, he clung close – he was in the preparation process and couldn't see being alone. His answer was, as you live and as your soul lives, I will not leave thee. But during the preparation, Elisha realized the separation was imminent. Ready or Not, Elijah was going up. Aware that this was it, Elisha asked for a double portion of Elijah's spirit. Elisha literally saw the separation and elevation and received his portion. He received what he'd prepared for.

When Jesus was in the garden of Gethsemane, he'd prepared his entire life for his glorious transformation. It was a separate experience. Jesus was not here on earth to have his own glory or show off his achievements or appear to be big and bad; rather, he came to do the will of the Father. Being crucified, beaten, whipped, scorned, and mocked wasn't a life of choice but was a part of God's divine purpose. Jesus knew his assignment and was prepared. He said, "If I am lifted up from the earth, I will draw all men unto me." (John 12:32 KJV). The process of separation was painful, but God's plan was and is to save us from our sins by Jesus' conquering death, hell, and the grave and to ascend back to the Father. If Jesus did not separate, we would not have the comforter. Separation doesn't feel good but must happen to accomplish God's will for your life.

Abraham had to separate from his family and all he knew before God would make his name great. Because we are under the Abrahamic covenant, that same blessing that was on Abraham is on us today. God said, "I will make you into a great nation, and I will bless you; I will make your name great, and you will be a blessing. I will bless those who bless you, and whoever curses you, I will curse" (Genesis 12:2-3 KJV). This message of dealing with a pest and separation rang true thousands of years ago, blessed the lives of many in 2007, and I pray it touches your heart today. If you believe God is calling you to go higher, say to yourself, "I'm Prepared to Be Elevated- I've been Separated to be Transformed."

Chapter 24: God's Plan is Generational

When you've been favored, you can't help but continue to win and have your life restored.

It all started when Joseph had a dream. Many times, when we dream about something good and actually remember it, we get excited and want to share. Not really giving much credence to the dream or its interpretation, just knowing this is what God showed us about our future, and we're excited about it. Genesis 37:5 NLT, "One night Joseph had a dream, and when he told his brothers about it, they hated him more than ever."

Joseph was already hated by his brothers, prior to his dream, for being his father's favorite which caused them to be out of control. "His brothers hated Joseph because their father loved him more than the rest of them. They couldn't say a kind word to him" (Genesis 37:4 NLT). Envy and jealousy had overtaken their hearts, and they plotted evil against him and were successful, or so they thought.

Because of their hatred towards their brother, Joseph suffered many things that he had no control over, but God was always in the midst. He was ridiculed by his brothers for his dreams, thrown into a pit, later sold as a slave, then accused of raping his master's wife, and ultimately thrown into prison. His brothers could care less about Joseph's future or his demise. They lied to his father and were happy (for a season) going through life without him. Even though Joseph was alone, with no family and no familiarity, God was still prospering him. The prison was blessed because of him; favor was all over his life.

Fast forward several years, there was a famine in the land. Joseph is taken out of prison and promoted to become second in command to his master. Joseph's brothers came to him for food, not knowing that the brother they hated and left for dead is now in a position of power to provide sustenance for them and their families. (I won't go through the entire story). Nevertheless, once Joseph reveals himself to his brothers, he does the unthinkable; he has them move close to him. He did not have to bless them, he did not owe them anything, but because of the heart that God put in him, he lived with integrity.

Joseph's dream came to pass. His father and the children of Israel were moved close to him so they wouldn't be affected by the famine. What his brothers meant for evil many years earlier was all a part of God's plan. This is our reminder that God's plans don't always feel good. Nevertheless, his plans will always work out for our good.

Even after the passing of Israel (Jacob – Joseph's father), Joseph reassures his brothers that he did not move them near him for payback. Joseph says, "Don't be afraid of me. Am I God, that I can punish you? You intended to harm me, but

God intended it all for good. He brought me to this position so I could save the lives of many people" (Genesis 50:19-20 NLT).

Throughout all the pain, the lies, the rejection, and the abandonment, Joseph comprehends that everything God orchestrates has a purpose. Joseph was taken from the people he knew and loved, even though they did not love him back. He was ultimately catapulted into his promise, living out his destiny and the dream God gave him many years earlier. He understood this good life was not just for him. Joseph understood that was the promise for that time, and God revealed future things to him.

You may be reading this and come from a close-knit family, that is commendable. However, there are some broken families out there. Some siblings hate each other because the father or mother loved one more than they loved the others through no fault of their own. You may have shared your dream and have been ostracized from your siblings or your parents due to the promise that God has given you.

It may be hard in the beginning, but you will long for those relationships. But just as God made Joseph forget the pain that he endured and continued to deliver and prosper Joseph, God will do the same for you. Envy and jealousy have crept into the hearts of many families because God has chosen to honor and exalt one above the other. However, that does not mean that God does not have a plan and purpose for everyone, just that some have been set apart a bit more than others.

Regardless, there will come a time when you are able to treat them the same way they treated you, but you must remember that you have been chosen by God, and this was all a part of his plan. I know you've been lied on, lied to, talked about, and left for dead. Even through that, what someone meant for evil in your life, God will use it for his good and fulfill his purpose. Romans 8:28, tells us, "That God causes everything to work together for the good of those who love God and are called according to his purpose for them" (NASB).

Understand that people are threatened by your potential, threatened that God is revealing himself to you and through you. Threatened that despite the opposition and the setbacks -you continue to win. The enemy is hoping that you don't fulfill the promise and will use your family or those close to you to irritate you, distract you and sow discord, and slander your name.

However, even during that, God will cause you to bless those who can never bless you back. Yep, God will have you bless those who despitefully use you and persecute you (Matthew 5:44 KJV). People who will never say thank you or who would ever be good to you even if they were able to. Yep, even those who front and act like they have this awesome two-way relationship with you, that is when they are with you; but hate you and everything you stand for behind your back. At that moment, you have two choices, be like them. Nope, you must continue to be obedient to God so you can continue to be blessed.

When you bless somebody, it's not about how they respond anyway. You must do what you are led to do, don't worry about the rest. God is using you to either meet a need or to plant a seed. Be obedient, so the blessings, favor, and grace of God continue to flourish in your life.

The famine reunited Joseph and his brothers. There is always purpose amid our pain. There was sorrow in the way in which his brothers treated him. They acknowledged their wrong and would have protected their younger brother Benjamin with their lives. We see reconciliation at work, and this, too, is a part of God's redemptive plan. God promised Abraham, Isaac, and Jacob a land of promise. Though they were no longer living, that promise was still in place and would be exemplified in the generations to come.

Whew! Once the famine was over, God revealed to Joseph things to come. So, the next time he shared a dream, a vision, or a premonition from God, his brothers listened attentively. Why? Because they saw Joseph's dream came to pass and how God used Joseph to preserve life, they knew this was the hand of God. Sibling rivalry had to flee, and the devices of the enemy had to bow to the plans and purposes of the Father. Even though the children of Israel were living comfortably and in abundance, that was the promise for their now but was not the promise for the generations thereafter. This was just a pit stop to the Promised Land.

Genesis 50: 24-25 NIV gives insight that this was not the promise for the children of Israel. "Soon I will die," Joseph told his brothers, "But God will surely come to help you and lead you out of this land of Egypt. He will bring you back to the land he solemnly promised to give to Abraham, to Isaac, and to Jacob." Then Joseph made the sons of Israel swear an oath, and he said, "When God comes to help you and lead you back, you must take my bones with you."

Fast forward several generations, there arose a new king over Egypt who did not know Joseph and the great works that God did through him (Exodus 1:8 NIV). Because this king did not know Joseph, he could care less about the Israelites and the favor God had on their lives. Come on now, how many times have you been in a position where you know it's the hand of God? You are up for a promotion at work, you have gone above and beyond for a project, and then a new supervisor comes in and says, I don't care what the person before me had in place. I want everyone to start with a clean slate.

You immediately question what is happening. God, you promised me this position, I've worked hard, and I've proven myself! Sometimes God is saying be patient, I am still working things out behind the scenes. Other times God is saying that promise is still going to come to pass for you, but not here. I want to take you to the place I have for you. Other times God is saying, go back and do what I told you five years ago. I have shown you my favor because you are my child, but I have greater. Don't lose sight of the best God has for you because you are satisfied with what's comfortable and familiar to you. Let God take you to your promised land.

Back in the Bible… we see the Israelites in heavy bondage and slavery, that is until Moses is called to approach Pharaoh. God purposely hardened Pharaoh's heart. Various plagues inconvenienced, hurt, killed, and caused unimaginable damage to the Egyptians.

When God wants to prune and separate, he will make a difference between whom he chooses. Exodus 9:4-6 NLT states, "The Lord will again make a distinction between the livestock of the Israelites and that of the Egyptians. Not a single one of Israel's animals will die! The Lord has already set the time for the plague to begin. He has declared that he will strike the land tomorrow. And the Lord did just as he had said. The next morning all the livestock of the Egyptians died, but the Israelites didn't lose a single animal".

If Pharaoh hadn't hardened his heart against the Israelites, surely all this destruction would not have come. Due to the continual preservation of Pharaoh and, most importantly, for God's word to come to pass, the chain of events was unleashed. When God puts his word or his stamp of approval on something, it's like a check you can take to the bank; it's good. God made a separation between the nations even though they were neighbors entwined together. But when God promises he will keep you, he will never leave you nor forsake you even during the opposition trust that God will do his thing.

When the children of Israel were finally free from their oppressor, Moses kept the word that Joseph gave generations before. Exodus 13:19 NIV states, "Moses took the bones of Joseph with him, for Joseph had made the sons of Israel swear to do this. He said, "God will certainly come to help you. When he does, you must take my bones with you from this place." Over four hundred years later, another part of the promise came to pass.

So, what does this mean for us today? This is a reminder not to let your children forget about their heritage and the generations before them. Don't forget where God has taken your family and where he promised to take you. It means that if God has spoken something over your life, whether it's a prophecy, a dream, a vision, or something that your grandmother prayed over your life, it will come to pass. It does not matter how long it takes, and it does not matter what the circumstances are, it doesn't matter how long you've been bound to a particular person, place, or thing. It doesn't matter who's for you or against you. What matters is when God speaks, his plan is set in motion, and what he promises will come to pass, not just for you but for your generations to come.

Chapter 25: Give God your all

Will you trust God and give him your all? As humans, we are okay with giving people just enough of us. Life has thrown many of us curve balls. We have made lemonade more times than we can count. We have tried to reshuffle the deck of cards we were given at birth, only to find ourselves withholding who we truly are to individuals. Many times, the blow of rejection, pain, hurt, scars, and trauma keep us guarded, and rightfully so at times. However, the blocked walls enable us from trusting and giving our all to anyone.

So, I know if we are guarding ourselves against people, we are guarding ourselves against God. God doesn't want you to block him out of your life. God sees, and he knows every setback and every victory. He wants you to leave your life at his feet, whether things are going good or bad. God wants all of you. So again, I'll ask will you trust God completely and give him your all?

To give your all to someone and to give your heart requires intimacy and trust on a whole nother level. Many times, I hear people say how much they trust God, but their trust has limitations. People still want to play God in some aspect of their lives. There is fear that God will move too slow or not at all; for this reason, many have been guilty of moving before God and really screwing up some things. So,

I'll ask, will you let your guard down and let God work on your heart?

This is what the Spirit of the Lord spoke to me: I have a lot in store for you. But, before I give you the miracle, before you see all the dreams and visions come to pass, I'll fulfill small requests and answers to prayers. I want to know if I can trust you with a little before I give you something big. Will you trust me and praise me over the seemingly insignificant details? Or will you take the little things for granted? Every door, every window, and every step is orchestrated in fulfilling the bigger things. I want to know if I can trust you with the small things before you reap the big harvest. I know you're waiting for me to perform the miraculous. I have power and want to show you things that your mind can't even comprehend. Trust me with all the details. Lean on me. I am the way. I am the truth. My ways are higher than yours. Trust my timing and trust my plan. Till the ground, I've given you. Cultivate it. I want to see you flourish. I want to see some fruit. I've been trimming people and situations in your life for a while now. I've been preparing you for ultimate surrender. I want your dependency on me. I want you to know that I am God, and above me, there is no other. The battles have been tougher than ever before. The fire has intensified, but purity in spirit is springing forth. You've been refined, you've been set apart. Look around, and you'll see I'm already overtaking you with my goodness. Trust me. Trust my will over yours. Let me be God. Let my word be the final authority. Look past today. See the vision again. My plan and purpose have stayed the same. You are the beacon of light. I need you sold out. Do not let your past haunt you, and do not allow your thoughts to destroy you. Submit to me, fully and unconditionally. Be consumed with me.

Chapter 26: Fight for your Life

Ready or Not, God has good things in store for you, but there are also stumbling blocks and divisions that you must overcome. Ready or not, you can do it and go through it. You are more than a conqueror. To be more than a conqueror means you will gain a decisive victory. This is a pronounced verdict from the Lord……. **YOU WILL OVERCOME!**

Understand you're in a battle – the fight for your life.

We must understand who the battle is with and who it's not with. The battle is not with each other; we are family and must operate in unity and show sincere and genuine love towards one another. The enemy will try to sow discord amongst the body of Christ – that is his job. Our job is to separate ourselves from that junk and tell the enemy he has no place with the believers of God.

Understand that the battleground is spiritual and is strongest in your mind. The enemy will try to turn you against yourself. Make you think people are saying things about you, whispering about you, and taunting you. The enemy will bring fear to try and rob you of peace and joy and have you listening to the voice of reason, ultimately overanalyzing what God says. Stop fighting yourself and the people around you, let God's words be so, be obedient, and don't milk the process.

So, who is the battle against? It's against satanic oppression, demonic spirits, and the powers of darkness. Ephesians 6:12 NIV states, "Our struggle is not against flesh and blood, but against the rulers, against the authorities, against the powers of this dark world and against the spiritual forces of evil in the heavenly realms."

How can you combat the powers of darkness? I'm glad you asked.

You must recognize you belong to El Elyon – which is God Most High. Recognizing whom you belong to gives a better glimpse of who you are. 1st Peter 2:9 NIV says, "You are Peculiar." To be peculiar means you are strange, odd, unusual, special, eccentric, belonging primarily to one person, group, or kind. Others recognize your unusualness, and therefore you stand out (and will never fit in). There are certain rights we have as special people, children of God, and heirs of Christ. We get benefits that the world cannot comprehend. You are a valuable possession belonging to God.

Not only are you royalty and set apart, but you are also a new creature. 2nd Corinthians 5:17 NIV says, "Therefore, if anyone is in Christ, the new creation has come. The old has gone, the new is here". We are restored and created new because of Christ. You must understand this transformation is spiritual. Our flesh must be denied, and our mind must be renewed. On the contrary, your spirit man is willing to live the life God designed. Your spirit is quickened, and understands that there's been a conversion. You have your Heavenly Father's DNA and the blood of Jesus flowing through your spiritual veins.

There are going to be times when you feel weak, unholy, and undeserving, but the Lord does not want you to have a defeated attitude, nor does he want you to believe the lies of the enemy. His strength is made perfect in our weakness (2 Corinthians 12:9 NIV). What you have to continually do is separate yourself. Why have you had so many difficulties? Why has your life been so hard? It was preparation for the good that's to come.

While I was going through some difficult times in my life, the Lord spoke in my spirit and said, "Smile – Count it all Joy – You are blessed and have been chosen to endure this, and at the end, you will speak." Whew! Is that word for anybody else out there?

Understand that the pain you endured was sent to purify you, cleanse you, and keep your mind, heart, and body in submission. People may try to remember what you were battling and what you had a hard time overcoming, but when you start walking in boldness and obedience, you won't have time for the haters because you'll be smiling as you count it all joy.

"Blessed are those who are persecuted because of righteousness, for theirs is the kingdom of heaven. Blessed are you when people insult you, persecute you and falsely say all kinds of evil against you because of me. Rejoice and be glad because great is your reward in heaven, for, in the same way, they persecuted the prophets who were before you." (Matthew 5:10-12 NIV).

We all go through challenges in our natural lives, and even more so when it comes to our faith. I've often heard it said that you are either going in a storm, in the middle of a storm or just coming out of a storm. What tests, trials, and storms teach us is that they will soon pass. Sometimes soon can't come fast enough. I get it. However, how we go through a situation is everything.

I've discovered 7 ways to Navigate a storm:

<u>Rest</u>

I know! I know! Rest is the furthest thing from our minds when we go through a storm. But resting does something for us in the natural and the spiritual realm. Rest shows that we are not overly concerned with the storm and that we are trusting God to bring us through. Meditating on the promises instead of the problem will bring such calm to your spirit. Matthew 11:28-29 NIV says, "Come to me, all you who are weary and burdened, and I will give you rest. Take my yoke upon you and learn from me, for I am gentle and humble in heart, and you will find rest for your souls."

Be Quiet

When you are going through a storm, you usually want to share with others. But every storm you're going through is not ready for an audience. You can stay in the storm longer by confiding in the very people that God is trying to pull you from. I encourage you to get quiet and spend time in prayer. Not everyone is ready for nor can handle your story. 1 Thessalonians 4:11 NIV says to "Study to be quiet." Let the Spirit guide you with whom to confide in, who to request prayer from and how much you should share.

Trust God

When you look at the circumstances or situations around you, it's easy to question God and even move ahead of his timing and plan. You're tired, you want to see change, and you don't understand what's happening. However, Isaiah 55:8-9 NIV says, "For my thoughts are not your thoughts, neither are your ways my ways, declares the Lord. As the heavens are higher than the earth, so are my ways higher than your ways and my thoughts than your thoughts." Trust that God's timing is always perfect. There's an old song I'm reminded of, "He may not come when we want him, but he's right on time."

<u>**Fear Not**</u>

Do not allow the storm to define you – you are just passing through. You will soon be over this one and can celebrate the victory before going to the next level God prepared for you. Don't be fearful, don't get stuck, don't lose heart, and don't shrink back. Continue to use your voice. "For the Spirit God gave us does not make us timid, but gives us power, love and self-discipline." (2 Timothy 1:7 NIV).

<u>**Be Bold**</u>

In every aspect of life – Confidence is Key. The psalmist David displayed great confidence, trust, and tenacity as he sought the Lord. He said, "When the wicked advance against me to devour me, it is my enemies and my foes who will stumble and fall. Though an army besieges me, my heart will not fear; though a war breaks out against me, even then, I will be confident." (Psalm 27:2-3 NIV). His boldness was in knowing that God would deliver him – God wants to deliver you when you come before him boldly.

<u>**Encourage Yourself**</u>

1st Samuel 30:6 NIV, we read that "David encouraged himself in the Lord." All the odds were stacked against him. At that defining moment in time, David had no allies. Have you ever been there? When nobody was around …. But God. Isaiah 41:10 NIV says, "So do not fear, for I am with you; do not be dismayed, for I am your God. I will strengthen you and help you; I will uphold you with my righteous right hand."

Be Thankful

One of the best things you can do is show gratitude. If you believe in the law of attraction, you understand that your positivity draws more positivity, and your negativity attracts more negativity. Having a grateful and thankful heart before you enter a storm, while you are in the storm and after you gain victory, shows God that he can trust you. When you are thankful- God goes from just taking care of the mundane in your life to making you complete and whole in him, lacking nothing. Let's be honest; we all can use some wholeness in our lives. In Luke 17, verses 11 – 19 NIV, Jesus healed ten lepers; but only one came back to say, "Thank You." Because of his gratitude, Jesus said to him, "Get up and go (on your way). Your faith (your personal trust in Me and your confidence in God's power has restored you to health." (V.19)

As you go through the storms of life, remember to Rest, be quiet, Trust God, Fear Not, Be Bold, encourage yourself, and Be Thankful. Know that God's working it out for your good in his time, God has plans to take you higher, but it does require steps on your part.

Chapter 27: This Battle Calls for Surrender

Surrender can often be expressed as giving up, throwing in the towel, or tapping out. When you think of surrender, your mind may quickly drift to opposition from an enemy. As humans with free will, there is no way that most of us are backing down from a fight or a competition. It is inherently in our DNA to win Sure, it may sound like an oxymoron, but keep reading.

When one thinks of the word surrender, it is associated with attributes of weakness. In a world where strength and fighting are a representation of prestige and glory, why would one ever give up or throw in the towel?

There is an aura of fight that is deeply embedded into each one of us. That sense of fight is necessary but can become overshadowed in the wrong situations. The enemy of our soul loves this confusion, loves this fight. If the enemy can keep you at war, he knows you will eventually grow tired, grow weary, become anxious, and eventually give up. Galatians 6:9 NIV, "Let us not become weary in doing good, for at the proper time we will reap a harvest if we do not give up."

Let me remind you again, that the heavy loads and burdens in your life were never meant for you to carry. In fact, Matthew 11:28-30 NIV is a reminder, "Come to me, all you who are weary and burdened, and I will give you rest. Take my yoke upon you and learn from me, for I am gentle and humble in heart, and you will find rest for your souls. For my yoke is easy, and my burden is light."

God wants you to come to him. God wants you to surrender to him. HE wants you to submit to HIS authority and HIS will for your life. God is not your enemy, but if you've been trained to believe that surrender is a dirty word or a sign of weakness, you will always be at odds between your flesh and your spirit man, and you will never surrender. You will continue operating in your own strength.

Surrender is such a strong word because it is a reminder that you DO NOT have to journey this life alone. There is peace and rest waiting for you when you stop trying to fight everything that comes against you in your own power.

YOU ARE IN A SPIRITUAL BATTLE. I know it's hard to remember to live life from a spiritual perspective when you are focused on what you can see and feel in the natural world. The spiritual world is more real, but if the enemy can keep you distracted, he will ensure you are in chaos trying to fight any and everybody over any and everything.

When you surrender to God, don't worry about it looking like the enemy has the upper hand. That situation you see is only temporary Continue to surrender to God. Trust in HIS Promises. Once your focus is intent on finding God's presence, peace and joy, the enemy will still be there, but his tactics won't be able to manipulate you as easily.

The goal in life is to not allow anything to hold you back from the plan, the promise, and the purpose that God has for your life. God is greater than anything, greater than any sickness, greater than any stronghold, and he is waiting for you to surrender to him. Though God specializes in miracles and suddenly changes the context of our lives, many times, we must wait it out, and that's alright too.

Understand that surrendering to God is not just a one-time thing. Surrender is a continual process, a conscience effort that you are giving up your will for God's. Surrendering to God is how you WIN in life, ultimately knowing that God's will is what's best for you. Will you surrender?

Chapter 28: Use your Weapons

I'd like to share five secrets with you today. Simply put- I want to tell you how to use your spiritual weapons. These secrets will help you no matter how you identify spiritually. So, if you consider yourself a baby in Christ, a believer, a Christian, a son/daughter of God, a seasoned saint, or someone seeking or desiring a relationship with our Heavenly Father, keep reading this is for you.

We've all heard that our weapons are not carnal, meaning we are not supposed to be fighting others in the flesh 2 Corinthians 10:4 NIV says, "The weapons we fight with are not the weapons of the world. On the contrary, they have divine power to demolish strongholds." So, when your back is up against the wall, you will see if you are going to fight with your flesh or if you are going to use your weapons. Are you using what you know, what you've been taught, and what you're sharing with others? Don't worry, you'll have plenty of opportunities to use your weapons.

So, what are the weapons I'm referring to? I'm so glad you asked. I'm referring to spiritual weapons. Here are the five secret weapons that many in the Bible had in their arsenal that allowed them to walk in victory.

Use your Hands – Not physically sock or slap someone. I know sometimes that may feel good but instead, use your hands by lifting them up. Lifting your hands is a sign of surrender. You are not surrendering to the enemy; mind you, you are surrendering to God. When you lift your hands, you are showing God that the battle belongs to him, and you are trusting him alone to deliver you. When you feel weak, know that God will sustain you. I am sent to remind you of the words found in Zechariah 4:6, "Not by might, nor by power, but by God's Spirit" Trust in God's ability; he has a proven track record and will not lose or fail you. Surrender to him!

Use your Voice – Not to vocally beat up others- or yourself- for not doing what you thought should've been done. Use your voice to speak life over your situations. Your situations may look stagnant, and spiritual death may gloom around individuals around you, but……this is your opportunity to bless and empower them to come up higher. If there is no support for you, you've got to learn to encourage yourself in the Lord. Speak the word over yourself; speak life over yourself. You don't need a cheerleader, a pastor, or an entourage. When it's late in the mid-night hour, and there is no one you can call on or depend on, you have got to learn to depend on God. 1 Samuel 30:6 NIV tells us about the great psalmist King David, and how he encouraged himself in the Lord. Since we have the power of the Holy Spirit living within us, we are equipped to use our voice, knowing that we have the mind of Christ (1 Corinthians 2:16 NIV).

Praise and Worship – Praise and Worship are not limited to the walls of a church, nor is it hindered by an online service. The praise and worship experience should swell in your heart and become a lifestyle. It takes time, I know, but it's not about what you show people. Praise and worship are what you are doing behind the scenes. At the end of the day, it doesn't matter if you are giving people a good show if your heart is not right. A life of praise and worship will turn your life around. I understand that there is nothing in this life that is perfect, But my God! Whew, I am reminded of the scripture, "Better is one day in your courts than a thousand elsewhere" (Psalm 84:10, NIV).

Prayer – Prayer is one of those underutilized gifts. Prayer is communion with God; we are all called to pray and intercede. There are common misconceptions that you need a Pastor, a Priest, or a Bishop to pray for you. That is a bondage mentality and a lazy and religious way of thinking. If you are saved and in relationship with God- **you are a minister of the gospel,** and you are just as equipped and have just as much authority and anointing to pray over a situation. It is going to require faith, growth, and trust, but when you are talking to and trusting in God's ability and not your own, you are guaranteed results. "Therefore, I tell you, whatever you ask for in prayer, believe that you have received it, and it will be yours" (Mark 11:24 NIV).

Thanksgiving – When your heart is grateful, you are thankful, appreciative, indebted, pleased, and ultimately filled with gratitude. Your heart is so full that grace exudes onto others around you. True thanksgiving starts with a heart aligned with God. Your vertical relationship will enlighten your horizontal relationships. Thanking God before you see answered prayers or a change in your life, your family's life, your marriage, your children, your job, or assignment is going to take an act of faith, but faith is also an act of worship and trust. Even when you feel like there is nothing to be grateful or thankful for, I want to assure you there is "Give thanks in all circumstances; for this is God's will for you in Christ Jesus" (1 Thessalonians 5:18, NIV).

You have weapons, and you have armor. Ephesians 6:10-18 NIV states, "Finally, be strong in the Lord and in his mighty power. Put on the full armor of God, so that you can take your stand against the devil's schemes. For our struggle is not against flesh and blood, but against the rulers, against the authorities, against the powers of this dark world, and against the spiritual forces of evil in the heavenly realms. Therefore, put on the full armor of God so that when the day of evil comes, you may be able to stand your ground, and after you have done everything, to stand. Stand firm then, with the belt of truth buckled around your waist, with the breastplate of righteousness in place, and with your feet fitted with the readiness that comes from the gospel of peace.

In addition to this, take up the shield of faith with which you can extinguish all the flaming arrows of the evil one. Take the helmet of salvation and the sword of the Spirit, which is the word of God. And pray in the Spirit on all occasions with all kinds of prayers and requests. With this in mind, be alert and always keep on praying for all the Lord's people."

The word of God is full of individuals who used these secret weapons to live an overcoming life, fulfilling their God-ordained plan and purpose. I love reading about King David because he used his hands, his voice, praise, worship, prayer, and thanksgiving. He was a man of war and specifically thanked God for teaching his hands to fight while he was under attack, before entering any battle, he sought God. He prayed and communed with God, praised and worshiped God, and thanked God. David was far from perfect like we are today, he killed an innocent man and was an adulterer, but even during his many shortcomings, God still said that David was a man after his heart. Why? Because he continually sought God, he continually trusted God, He continually used his spiritual weapons, he was armed, and God blessed him despite it all.

Chapter 29: That Place called Peace

I have been on a journey searching for inner peace for some time now. The more I desire peace, the more I see that there are things, people, situations, and environments that are not conducive to what I am seeking after. The more I crave and follow after God, the more I am willing to say goodbye to what's not for me.

The more my soul desires peace, the more I let go of things that are truly not for me.

It's like my subconscious is speaking to the universe and telling my spirit it's time to be free.

Unglued from the distractions that once held me captive,

Aligned with the vision that's flowing so rapid.

Immersed with old dreams and new insights, it's amazing.

What your soul and spirit hear when the world it's not craving.

The joy in my spirit, the song in my soul, the knowingness and certainty of becoming whole.

All happened when I became intentional of the release, knowing at the very least I deserved inner peace.

The casualties of friendships and relationships after that point,

Hurt for only a moment when I realized this was my greatest choice.

I stopped begging, I stopped asking for the doors I saw that were closing,

Knowing that God has greater for me, I gave him all, withholding nothing.

I learned to give God the best of me, more than simply what was left of me.

It was time for my agenda to take a back seat to the power and purpose that was destined for me.

These awakening moments hit us all from time to time, but if we stay intentional, we will indeed gain the prize.

It's time to stay woke, no more drifting off to sleep, it's your moment, it's your time, claim your peace and release.

There is a place that is so tranquil, so beautiful, so freeing. You can't book a vacation there, but you can go there as often as you like. That place is a place called peace. Once you get there, you will never want to leave, and you'll want to protect your peace at all costs. In my younger years, I would try to let my mind journey there. Throughout all the chaos I experienced in my life, singing a song, meditating, writing, and enjoying the stillness would bring peace. The peace, however, would be short-lived. I hadn't learned to master a peaceful state of mind. When my circumstances changed, my peace would sometimes fly out of the window.

The older I've gotten, I still experience chaos to some extent. I've learned that I can only control my personal environment, and with the state of our world and personal lives, we get to choose how we respond. Adulting brings on overwhelming tendencies of anxiousness because there is so much on the line. You have people looking up to you and generational blessings that you want to pass on to them. So, trying to perfect this thing called life is always at the forefront of our minds.

There is still daily life, working, paying bills, marriage, children, cleaning the house, and building what God has given to you. Disagreements come, friends and family move on, the stress of wondering how you will survive one more thing, and then you realize that amongst it all, you are smiling and still have joy. You are not worried about what's next. You are not frantic about what to do, who to call. Instead, you take a deep breath, pray and Trust that God will keep his word to you and do what he promised.

That is a place I want all of you to get to. Some of you may already be there; that place is a place of peace. Yes, you may cry a few tears because life can hurt, but instead of staying in a place that is unhealthy, you decide you are giving it all over to God. The peace he fills your heart with when you do this is indescribable.

When I think of this kind of peace, I think of John 14:27 NIV, when Jesus said, "Peace I leave with you; my peace I give you. I do not give to you as the world gives. Do not let your hearts be troubled, and do not be afraid."

Such power lies in those words. The peace that God gives the world doesn't quite understand. How could you lose your job and still believe that you will be blessed with something greater? You may be going through a divorce and not necessarily happy with the demise of your marriage, but you have the peace of knowing that God brought you this far and will never leave you. You may be struggling with a medical condition but continue trusting that the same God who healed you before will heal you again.

On the outside, the world doesn't quite understand this peace. When a loved one passes, when you watch drugs try to destroy those close to you, it is imagined that you will break down in a state of depression or question the love of God. The most important thing to realize is that everything is not God. So don't go back to drinking or damaging your body to find temporary peace. Understand that everything is not a punishment. Instead of shutting God out, this is a time to draw nearer than ever before and not only visit but live in a state of perpetual peace.

Peace can be challenged on huge levels, as we read above, but what about the rude people you encounter doing the seemingly mundane? Getting cut off on the freeway, a rude person at the store, or on the phone while you are handling business. Yep, you want to maintain your peace at all costs. Peace is a precious commodity. Though everyone around you can be in a state of unrest, you have the power to rise above it all.

This doesn't mean that you won't be bothered or upset about a person's actions towards you, nor does it mean that you will lie down and take abuse. What it does mean is that you will check your heart and not respond the way you used to. In fact, in those situations that you used to have no self-control over and could almost never contain yourself, you will notice that as you grow deeper, it's like water off a duck's back. That is a place of peace.

Others may not understand who you are becoming and what the change is about, and sometimes you may not quite understand it either. It is a call to go higher, a call to go deeper. It is a call to live in a place so freeing that you don't ever want to go back to any type of bull.

Once you experience this peace, you will protect it at all costs. That means you will set your house in order. Understanding you set the tone for your home and are more powerful than you could ever imagine. Who cares if they want to live wild and crazy? You can still have a peaceful home and haven. In fact, when your family watches your new God-given response, they can't help but notice something is different and want to live in this perpetual state of peace as well. Or maybe they'll think your weird, but regardless your response will stay the same.

I encourage you to pray over your home. Pray over your children. If they aren't home, touch their picture, speak their names, touch an old bedroom door. Anoint your home. Sweep the mess and the chaos out. Burn sage, put a drop of oil in your hands, and anoint your doors.

One of my friends and neighbors told me she goes one step further. She walks the line of her property and prays over it. She calls it the bloodline. So not only is she believing God to protect what and who is in her home, she believes that no harm and devastation will pass her driveway. That is faith, trust, and peace of mind.

A few months ago, there was a robber in my neighborhood. My husband came home from work and noticed my door and trunk were open and thought I had forgotten to close them. So, he closed it and didn't think too much of it. I distinctly remembered closing both. We checked our cameras, and low and behold, someone came to my home around 3 in the morning, opened my door (which I did forget to lock), popped my trunk open, and he looked up right into my cameras, got spooked and ran off.

What we would find out later was that he did this to everyone in our neighborhood. Taking paperwork, phone chargers, purses, whatever he could find. To be honest, my peace was a bit shot, and I felt violated. We've had cameras for over 8 years, our home is well lit, but my husband made it even brighter, putting out more lights and cameras. My husband spares no expense when it comes to protecting and ensuring the safety of his family. Let me let you in on a secret. God will do the same for you when it comes to you experiencing HIS peace.

I felt bad for the people with the fake cameras or just the ring because it didn't pick up much. Everyone in the neighborhood knows who has the real thing and usually comes to us and others for help with the police, showing recordings and such if something arises. This is rare, but it happens. My friend, who rarely leaves her porch light on, didn't have it on that night either, but I believe that bloodline of prayer protected her. Her things were ruffled through, but nothing was taken.

The attacks still come, and no one is immune from life happening. The word of God declares, "The weapon can form against us, it just won't be able to prosper" (Isaiah 54:17 NIV).

Just as we want peace of mind for our homes and our families, we want to have that same peace of mind in our hearts and mind. We don't want to be disturbed by every event that is brought to shake us up. Your soul can believe God, and your flesh will still respond how it wants. It's natural to respond angrily but do something about it. Don't just do temporary things that are fleeting but protect your peace at all costs. That's a place where you dwell, where others want to be, and will soon ask you how to get there.

Let me tell you, I did pray over my oil, and I did go outside with the bottle of oil and walked around the perimeter of my home. It was early in the morning. Bonnet on with pajamas and flip-flops, but I anointed the curb, the cars, the grass, and the rocks. A few neighbors looked at me weirdly, but I continued to put a line of separation with what God personally entrusted to me. I anoint the inside of my home all the time but placing that bloodline around my property gave me more peace. It doesn't matter if you live in a mansion or an apartment. God will protect what he's entrusted to you.

Chapter 30: Keep Going – Don't Abort your Destiny

As we move to the precipice of where God is taking us, it is important that we keep our focus on him and listen to the still, small voice. God is always speaking to us, but if we don't have ears ready to hear, then we will miss out on what he is trying to say. You may be hearing the voice of God good one day and then feel like your spiritual connection drops the next. We've all been there in the spiritual and in the natural. We have all experienced a dropped call in our lives. If we want to hear what someone has to say, we call back, but when we don't, we just let that call go.

To fully hone into the call, discernment is going to be key. We need to discern who God wants in our life, how to spend our days and time, and when to move. I believe that God will speak to you specifically, as he has done for so many countless others through the word of God. It is important that we don't ignore the nudges and the warnings that we hear. When we do, we can generally find ourselves hurt or in situations that are hard to get out off.

When you are on the path that God ordained for you, that's when the enemy comes along to try to get you to abort your destiny. I'm here to remind you: Do Not Abort your Destiny! Jesus was our perfect example of persistence. If you just keep going, keep pushing, you will reach your destiny.

The enemy wants nothing more than to distract you from hearing God's voice. Their goal is to get you to never accomplish God's will for your life. The enemy comes for you and tempts you at your weakest when you are hungry.

If you've ever fasted for more than 2 days, you know you can't just go have a steak; you will hurt yourself. You need to ease back into solid food and start with broth or soup. But when you're starving, you will grab something that your stomach can't handle. The same emotionally. What have you been starving for? Has it been affection, attention, friendship, or recognition? Whatever you are physically lacking, the enemy slides on through to tempt you. You've seen a vision, a dream, and are trying to make a prophecy happen like yesterday, and the enemy is subtle. His tactics look innocent. The devil wants nothing more than to make a fool of you. All the while, God is speaking, "no, don't" "move," "do this instead," don't be enticed by what you see.

Understand that life gets hardest right before the breakthrough. The time of most resistance comes right before the release. Keep going; you can slow down if you must, you can sit down if you must, take a break, fix your face, dry your tears, and then get back to what you were working on and believing God for. Continually speak positive things in the atmosphere. I don't care what it looks like, speak those things that are not as though they were. You need positivity in the atmosphere, you set the tone for what you want in your life. You have the power to decree and declare a thing.

It may feel like you go from one obstacle to another. You may wonder how much more you can take but remember, as hard as it gets at times, you are not going through things for yourself. You have been called and set apart to help somebody else. You hold the key, but you have got to keep going so you can unlock the door of greatness that lies ahead. The doors you open, the barriers you break, will allow countless others to be free. You may not be able to see it just yet, but it's there. Keep going, don't give up.

You have got to persevere, be determined, and stay focused. To persevere means to persist despite counter influences, opposition, or discouragement. To be determined means you've made a firm decision, and you are resolved not to change it. To be focused is to fix your attention on your goals, on your desires, and eliminate anything or anyone who would keep you from your God-given purpose. I shouldn't say if, but when you have moments that you've let the day get the best of you, don't sit there, and have a pity party, get back up.

Life is not going to wait for you and your circumstances to be perfect. You have your destiny to fulfill and a mark to leave on this earth. It's going to be up to you, though. People will come into your life when you are in a time of transition. They won't understand you, nor try to. They may even be offended by you. They may be overly sensitive and critical of everything you try to do or even the things you aren't doing. Don't continually try to explain yourself and persuade your point of view. You've been there and have done that in your past. You've got to keep moving in your future, with or without them. Please don't let unhealthy people repeatedly bring you down. You left them alone for a reason, don't go back. You've got to move into your future.

As much as you want to, you can't help everybody. It may sound selfish, but the reality is you've got to help yourself; you've got to do what God has purposed in your heart to do. You will never have peace and walk on purpose, wondering what everyone around you thinks. Know that God is up to something good. Just because you can't see it does not mean it is not happening in the spirit and getting ready to propel you into the actual world.

Today I believe that God is looking at you and saying you are still a person of value. You are still a man/woman after my heart. The thief (enemy) can see your potential and sees how great you are years before you begin to even acknowledge that there is greatness in you. The goal of the enemy is that you never reach your potential. If he can steal your peace, your joy, your love, your trust, your compassion, he can infiltrate your heart. If he can kill your vision and get you to abort God's plan before you understand your why and your purpose, he can keep you defeated and going around in circles. The enemy will use whoever or whatever he can to try to get you to quit, try to get you to back down, or get under your skin.

God wants you to live an abundant life, both now and the hereafter. God wants you to live full of peace and purpose. Full of joy that overflows and impacts not just your life but the lives of those you encounter. God wants you to live abundantly. Can you envision a loving father wanting only the best for you? If you grew up without a father, it could be hard to understand the love of your Heavenly Father. It took me years to accept God's love, but when I embraced that God loved me unconditionally, it was freeing. God loves you unconditionally too.

The enemy is jealous. Why? Because he desires that type of relationship and will lie and deceive you into believing how unloved and how unworthy you are. If the enemy can't have a decent relationship with God, he doesn't want you to have one either. Today I challenge you to push past the lies. Every time a negative comment creeps in, I want you to recognize that it is not the voice of your heavenly father. That is the voice of a thief, and we do not have time to let a thief take what rightfully belongs to us.

Just as you protect your home or car by locking it and setting the alarm, you protect your heart when you realize you are no longer going to allow the foolishness. Are you ready for overflow? Are you ready to work out what's in you? It's time for you to think, walk and live abundantly.

Learn to discern God's voice.

Don't fall for the lies and the traps set out by the enemy.

Believe that you deserve God's best.

Have an abundant mentality.

I believe that overflow is on its way. The last few years or months may have been hard for you, but I believe that the tide is changing in your favor. Get ready for it!

Let's Pray: Holy Spirit equip me to have ears to hear and eyes to see the devices of the enemy. Allow me to hear your voice and trust your plan. Let me not be anxious about what I don't understand, but trust in your timing, your voice, and what you've promised me. Lord, I trust you and will not abort the destiny you've assigned to me. In Jesus' Name ~Amen

Chapter 31: Step Away from your Comfort Zone

There is a move and a shift coming, but to walk in that shift, you must step away from your comfort zone. I believe you are entering a new season of unchartered territory. A season of open doors and a season where you can't do business as usual.

Let me first say that Anything with the word comfort in it has a warm and cozy connotation to it for me. When I eat comfort food, I get this happy, warm, and fuzzy feeling. When I cuddle in my recliner with my blanket wrapped around me ever so snugly, I feel warmth, peace, and comfort. There is comfort in familiarity, such comfort that it can keep us from ever stepping out.

Being comfortable is a good thing. We tend to interact with those who bring us comfort. Comfort, as wonderful as it is, can have some drawbacks. Sometimes we get so comfortable in being alone that we don't embrace new relationships. We get so comfortable in a job that we get scared to start a business. We are so used to things being just the way they are. We are warm and cozy and don't want anyone or anything to disrupt that feeling.

You may start a new exercise routine or change your eating habits and slowly revert to your old habits. Why? Because it's comfortable. We want the change without the commitment. Commitment requires extra effort on our part. It makes us step out in the cold, step out on faith, and trust God like we never have before.

If you are finding yourself wanting more but feel a bit stuck because of things that happened in the past, I want you to take time and do a bit of self-reflection and soul searching. Ask yourself why you feel the way you do? What can you do to bring about change? And then I want you to step out and do something different.

What results do you want to see in your life, and with your family? Just because there is comfort in a thing does not make it good or healthy for you. What may have been good and worked well last year may not yield the same results right now. If this resonates with you, I want to encourage you to step away from your comfort zone.

You are going to be ok. Once you get over the preconceived ideas you have and start pushing forward, you will realize that this next step aligns with your destiny. It's almost like you were held back for a season (on purpose), but now you are going to be launched into the unknown.

It may seem a bit scary, this is new ground, but I promise you that God will be with you every step of the way, and you are going to be so glad that you stepped away from the things that kept you bound. Don't allow anyone to keep you comfortable and quiet when it's your time to stand up, speak up, and stand out. Know that God has prepared the way for you.

Detours to destiny are unavoidable, and they are often beyond our control. Sometimes we can circumvent them by ensuring our lives are in alignment with what our Heavenly Father already told us and set out for us. Pay attention to your daily encounters, and see what is causing a distraction or delay in your purpose. Write down what people, what things, or what situations throw your life or your day off course. Are you able to avoid any of them? How can you minimize engagement? What motivates you and keeps you focused?

Chapter 32: Moving Ahead of God

Growing up as a little girl in church, my late grandfather Dr. Robert Thrash Sr., would quote either Malachi 3:8 -12 or Luke 6:38 at offering time. I can still hear his voice intermittently saying, "Will a man rob God, yet he has robbed me" – "Give and it shall be given unto you" – "I will rebuke the devourer for your sakes." As a child, I understood the concept of sowing and reaping, and it was ingrained in my heart to be a giver. I learned to give God back financially what he had entrusted to me. However, it was hard to give him my all and give him my heart. I recognized him as Savior, but Lordship was something I wasn't ready for.

God didn't always move the way I wanted him to or the way I needed him to, so I tried to help him out.

Abraham was a prime example of moving ahead of God's timetable. He had a word from God, but he couldn't see it. He was getting older, perhaps a bit impatient, and he wanted the promise of God to come to pass – like yesterday. Have you been there? Don't get me wrong, Abraham loved God, he trusted God, but he also moved ahead of God's timing, like many of us. God said, "Look up at the sky and count the stars – if indeed you can count them, so shall your offspring be" (Genesis 15:5 NIV). Many of you know the story- Abraham's wife Sarah convinced him to have a child with her maid Hagar (Genesis 16:4 NIV). Sarah later grew jealous (who wouldn't) and regretted her decision.

Though both Abraham and Sarah moved ahead of God, God still blessed them. In fact, God blessed the child born with Hagar, but the promise was on the child that he and Sarah would have. Regardless of them moving ahead of God's timing, they still had to wait on the promise. Waiting requires trust.

You must be patient and allow God space to work. Like Abraham, like Sarah, like me, and countless others, you will be challenged to move ahead of God. Daily, weekly, monthly, yearly, God will challenge you…... Do you still trust me completely? Do you still trust me with your marriage, your health, your children, your business, your ministry, your house, your car, your money, your family, your job, and your friendships? Will you be moved by what you see, or will you patiently wait? It is hard to wait patiently when nothing around you seems to make much sense. Sometimes it's easier to throw your hands up and walk away or try to fix it. God is saying - Throw your hands up in surrender and watch him work.

I brought up the concept of tithe and offering because when we give – God rebukes the devourer for our sakes. He opens the windows of heaven and pours out blessings that there is not room enough to receive. The devourer wants to destroy every aspect of your life. But when you give, the windows of heaven are opened. That doesn't mean that you will always receive a financial blessing, but you will receive what you need. Some of you may need your child off drugs and to return home. Some may need your marriage restored, and some may need both physical and mental healing. Go ahead now and tell God what you need! Do not limit God. Trust him and give him the space to work. Trust him in the process.

Now I want to revisit Abraham for a minute. God blessed Abraham and Sarah with the promised child Isaac, but can you believe he was challenged, tested, and tempted once again? God wanted to see if Abraham would be willing to give him everything and asked him to sacrifice his son. The promised son. By this time, Abraham was done with moving ahead of God. When he was willing to let go of the promise, God knew that his heart was real. Genesis 22:12 NIV says, "Do not lay a hand on the boy, do not do anything to him. Now I know that you fear God because you have not withheld from me your son, your only son."

God wants to move in your life so freely, and he is waiting for you to give him your all. HE wants to be Lord over every aspect of your life. God does not want you guarded with him; he does not want you protective over what he has blessed you with. He wants you willing to lose it all, so he can bless you far greater than you've ever imagined. Know that whatever you are going through, this too shall pass.

When my daughter was having a hard time recovering from the trauma of her past, I was there watching her like a hawk. Praying for her, encouraging her, speaking life into her.

She didn't always want me there, but there I was anyway. There would be times when the enemy would rear his ugly head in her life, and I felt that I had to save her from herself. One night, God told me to let go. Because I suffered from abandonment issues and I was living triggered, I didn't want to let go, I wanted to be there for her.

God reminded me that though she was my natural daughter, she was his daughter too. He showed me that our needs were entirely different, and she didn't need what I needed. God showed me how to nurture her by listening to her needs. Now, of course, my children had freedom, but if I felt like there was danger, I was a momma bear in protection mode. Her healing wouldn't come the way I wanted it to, nor the way I wished it would've come for me. My being her mother, advocate, and supporter was enough. I could not try to play God in her life, and I had to trust the master to do his job.

"If you love your father or mother more than you love me, you are not worthy of being mine; or if you love your son or daughter more than me, you are not worthy of being mine" (Matthew 10:37 NLT).

It was hard for me to walk away. My heart was hurting, it was breaking, but God wanted to know if he could trust me and if I would give her up for him. I went into my room and cried out and prayed. I was in anguish, I wanted to have peace over the situation, and I was determined to trust God. I struggled to grasp what that meant at the moment, but I had to stand on what God promised me for her life years prior. This was something that God had to do in and through her.

I knew that night I was getting nowhere. I had to let go, I had to walk away, I had to trust God. God used that moment to show my daughter that HE was for her and that he would never leave her, despite what she'd gone through. He loved her just as much, if not more than I did, and he would ensure she was okay. God used that moment to remind me that He has control of the situation.

Whatever is hindering you, whatever you feel like you must control for your life to function, I challenge you to leave it at the feet of Jesus. Are you willing to let go of the promise? Let it or them Go! God always has a ram in the bush as he did for Abraham, for Isaac, and for me. It may take longer than you expected. You may have some nights where you cried so much you feel there are no tears left. I challenge you to leave it at God's feet. Let God work it out. Stop moving ahead of God, give God the time and space to work, and watch what he does in your life when you continually trust him and give him your all.

Chapter 33: Cracked but still Usable

Generally, when I prepare eggs, I crack them in a separate bowl and whisk them before pouring them into my skillet. When I'm in a rush, all bets are off. I can generally be found cracking eggs on the stove or on the side of the skillet, and into the skillet they go. Yesterday was one of those "I'm in a rush kinds of days." Everything was going well until I got to my very last egg. Somehow, the entire egg flew from my hand and was on its way to the floor. I'm literally watching this happen in slow motion, but my hands can't move fast enough to grab it. Yep, it was one of those mornings.

Now, as I'm waiting to hear this splat on the floor, I realize there's no sound nor any egg oozing near my feet. By this time, I am searching for the egg frantically so I don't burn what I already have in my skillet. Mysteriously, the egg got stuck on the corner handle of the oven. Bizarre, I know! It was barely cracked. Imagine me, one moment waiting for yolk to be all over my kitchen floor and become a glob of worthless slime, but somehow it was preserved, and though it was cracked, though it was flawed, it was still whole. The outer shell was barely cracked, and the membrane was still intact. I was able to still use this egg that just seconds ago I counted out.

This egg reminded me of life in general. Sometimes we are in a rush and don't put a lot of thought into what's happening around us or how it will affect us. We are all fragile like this egg; we have a lot going on. The next thing you know, we have fallen, and we feel like our lives are over. We think we are finished; we're destroyed. But God catches us and doesn't let us fall all the way. We may be harboring embarrassment; we may have guilt and feel ashamed because we've fallen. However, the grace of God catches us, and his love covers us.

We may suffer some emotional and physical consequences of our spiritual and natural fall, and maybe some people watched us go down. Through this, Proverbs 24:16-18 NIV, reads, "Though the righteous fall seven times, they rise again, but the wicked stumble when calamity strikes. Do not gloat when your enemy falls; when they stumble, do not let your heart rejoice, or the Lord will see and disapprove and turn his wrath away from them".

Even though you are broken, you are still intact enough to be used for God's glory. You have not been counted out. In fact, God loves using broken, imperfect people to fulfill his plan and purpose on this earth. So please don't beat yourself up, nor stay in the position you're in. Thank God for catching you! Identify and repent of what caused the fall, and understand you are still able to be used, still considered worthy, still considered righteous, and most importantly, you are still loved.

King David is one of my favorite people to read about in the scriptures. He was a man who trusted God, but he was also a man that made several mistakes, big and small. He knew that true repentance was his key to victory. He said, "My sacrifice, O God, is a broken spirit; a broken and contrite heart you, God, will not despise" (Psalm 51:17 NIV). Once he repented for his many flaws, his many falls, he would get up and regain his place back in the kingdom as King.

Understand that your life did not catch God by surprise. He knows your ending from the beginning. Every fall, every mistake, is a part of God's plan. Do not let your fall, no matter how many times you've fallen, be indicative of your future and what God has promised to do in your life. God still wants to use you as a part of Kingdom building, go back to your place of royalty and make the devil mad.

You can do this; God's got you, he is with you, and I am rooting for you. Just like I was able to use my egg and go on and make breakfast for my family, God is still able to use you for his glory. Let me let you in on a secret, not one person living on this earth is perfect. Not one person is without sin. Not one person hasn't fallen. Therefore, we rely on Jesus! He graciously repairs our brokenness and puts us back together again. Thank God for the great King, King Jesus, who can restore us and put us back together again.

Chapter 34: Stay Connected

For much of anything to function in this world, it must be connected to something greater than itself. Something small always needs something greater to enrich it, nurture it, and restore its balance. Seeds need fertile soil, or one will never reap a full harvest. Flowers need water and to be pruned, or they will never flourish and will eventually fade away. Cars need gas or electricity, or you will be running empty. Yin needs Yang, and collard greens need cornbread (that was part of last night's dinner); I think you get my point. One thing does not work well without the other. These examples are all constants in life, they can go stretches of time without being full of any of the opposing components listed above, but ultimately everything needs to connect to something.

The other day I forgot to charge my phone. I thought to myself, big deal, I could give it a quick charge in the morning and be okay for the day. However, as I was getting ready for my day, I didn't remember to put the phone on the charger, and the next thing you know, the day started to get away from me. I was on my phone for meetings, appointments, and leisure and then noticed my phone was about to die. I needed to get to a charger and pronto. What I realized next really baffled me for a bit. I had been sitting right next to a charger the entire time and simply forgot to connect to it.

This brings me back to the beginning - to reach the full capability of anything in life, everything needs to be connected to a source of a power stronger than itself.

My phone looked good on the outside, but internally it was worn out, tired, and about to give up because it was not connected. If you've ever had your phone on the last few bars or on a few percent, you understand the dire need to connect, especially if you are in the middle of a meeting; you can't afford for your phone to die. Or worse, you depend on the map on your phone for directional guidance, and right when you need your phone to work the most, it dies. It could take a while sometimes for your phone to load, and you may have to wait for your contacts to sync. This can be annoying if you're waiting to get back on a zoom call, and if you are using the map app, you may be taking the wrong turns or must pull over to the side of the road waiting for a signal. Depending on your phone and your carrier, it could be a matter of seconds or a matter of minutes before you are back where you need to be. (Am I the only one this has ever happened to?)

As I reflected on my phone and the charger sitting next to me, I thought about our spiritual lives. On the outside, we look good, we smell good, our hair is on point, and we know what to say and when to say it. We are so busy running around and taking care of business, our families, and trying to save face that we forget that we are both spirit and natural beings that need to connect and get charged by the power source. As great and as strong as we are, we still need to connect to something greater than ourselves. Being connected and staying charged is going to be so important for the rest of your life. DO NOT let your spiritual battery run low or, worse, die. You can always reconnect, but if you've set your goals out for your life and you believe God to show up in your life, you have got to get connected and stay connected to the POWER Source.

Take the lessons learned from the past into your future. If we are all honest with ourselves, none of us want to go through some of the tests and trials that we experienced last year or years prior. We must celebrate the good that has come through our lessons learned and allow the positive aspects to propel us, even if the most positive lesson was to never get involved in something specific again. This awareness will be necessary. Some of the greatest things I learned in my past was to be even more intentional than I was before. I learned to slow down and to let go of what wasn't for me (no matter how great it seemed). Obedience, focus, and discipline are going to be great characteristics to move you into your purpose.

The most important step in journeying to your destiny is staying humble. Keep in mind, if a person is telling you how humble they are, they usually aren't. A humble person will not have to announce humility as it is seen and experienced by others. When you start flowing in your purpose, and your big strides are noticeable, please be excited, please share with others, and please help others. But DO NOT look down on others for tripping on the same steps that you failed on in your journey. DO NOT frown your nose at someone who is experiencing detours that are beyond their control. DO NOT think that you've arrived and you are the absolute best. You will want to keep your heart humble before God so you are not humbled and lose what you've worked so hard for.

When you encounter individuals falling into similar traps that you once fell into, you generally want to help them not make the same mistakes. That is for those who genuinely love others. Some may fall several times because the trap that enticed them once has a different look, a different feel; however, wisdom is the discerning force that will say, "HEY, don't keep falling for the okey-doke." You've been here before; get up, go home, pick up the pieces, and pass the test.

As you continually seek the face of God and listen for his still small voice, it's going to cost you something. It will cost you turning down engagements, putting your phone on silent, giving your social media a break, and ultimately saying NO to the things that demand your attention and time but have no true reward. It will cost you to live with intention, live with discipline and continually seek the face of God. Not the hand of God, not the "gimmie" mentality that lurks in our society, but true intimacy.

Those in relationships know that the "gimmie" mentality is fleeting. When someone only wants you for what you can offer without anything in return, you pump the breaks and reevaluate the relationship. But when someone genuinely wants to be around you, learn from you, talk to you, and truly listen, you want to give them the world. This is true for families, friendships, and marriages, and our relationship with God is no different.

I know that God wants to do more than you could ever imagine. If HE has shown you a glimpse of your future, know that your future is going to be so much greater than what you can see, think, or imagine. The world awaits you; the sky is the limit. God wants you to take back your spiritual dominion, but it's going to take seeking God to keep your authority. It's going to take wisdom to navigate the plans and purpose set out for you. It's going to take being alone sometimes, not sharing popular opinions, not worrying about who doesn't like the new you that you are embracing. It's going to take a made-up mind.

It takes no practice to remain childish and foolish and to remain stagnate. However, it will take everything in you to grow in wisdom, maturity, and strength. You are already different, you have already been set apart, and you don't fit in with the culture no matter how hard you try. You've been divinely created to serve a higher purpose. You are royalty! Will you stay connected to God and detach yourself from what's been hindering you?

Staying connected and having a strong spiritual battery keeps you grateful, aware of your surroundings, and content in where you are though you are striving for more. Staying connected to the power source allows you to be supportive and compassionate, and you can hear and discern a lot clearer. When your spiritual battery is on the last leg, you are frantic, only concerned about your needs, easily offended, upset with others for the smallest thing, complaining, and ready to connect to anything no matter if the plug fits or not. In these times of desperation to connect to POWER, we find that we are susceptible to advise, directions, and suggestions that our spiritually charged self would have never listened to.

I encourage you to stay connected, stay grounded, stay positive, and determined. There will be many opportunities to try to get you to think otherwise, to attempt to drain your battery, but you already know what to do. Proverbs 3:5-6 NIV says to "Trust in the Lord with all your heart, and lean not on your own understanding; in all your ways submit to him, and he will make your paths straight."

When you are presented with an opportunity, pray before you say Yes. Ensure that you've heard from God, whether the answer is yes, no, or wait. Do not move on to that thing, no matter how good it sounds, until you have your answer. Don't let your fear, insecurities, lack, or greed make your mind up for you. Do not let someone sweet talk you, pressure or convince you to move before you are in alignment with your purpose.

Chapter 35: You can Pass the Test

The Lords designed you to pass the test, and once complete, you enter his rest. In this test, he's appointed an open book. To pass, you need only to look. What should you do in a wilderness experience? This desolate place is one comprised of temptations, trials, and tests. You will face many obstacles as you walk through the wilderness. There are many natural components of going through, such as loneliness, separation, greed, being high-minded, lust, coveting, anger, and even depression and anxiety.

Our wilderness experience is allowed by God for spiritual growth and natural development. Life is not always fair. The trauma you've experienced may not be your fault. However, if you have never experienced the storms of life, you could not fully appreciate the best God has for you. The wilderness experience humbles you and allows God to be glorified in your life. Walking through the wilderness can be therapeutic if you learn to let go of the past and take off the masks. You don't have to act like you've got it all together. God can't heal what you won't reveal, so take it to God; he can handle it.

I grew up enduring a lot of abuse. This abuse was not limited to home, but to churches I attended, people who were supposed to be for me. I grew up in church, and abuse was not a topic that was discussed. You had to act like everything was perfect. There was fear of judgment and ridicule by the congregation and more so from family.

There were things you just didn't talk about. No one wanted to prove to be a stereotype, and so I learned to live masked. I watched others live masked.

If we are honest with ourselves, we have all worn masks at one time or another. The mask could be to hide insecurities or failures. Sometimes the mask is worn so long that you start to even fool yourself. As you go through this season of life, through this wilderness experience, take the mask off and be free. God can handle the real you.

You don't have to fake behind a persona of what others feel you should be. You don't have to hide behind your scars and imperfections. It's ok to talk to someone about your life, and most importantly, you can give your life completely over to God. He loves you and will care for you.

A pig who wallows to cool itself in the trenches is like a person who's masquerading while in an emotional ditch.

At moments it's comforting and may feel like bliss until you are alone and have time to reminisce.

Suddenly you gain composure and try to straighten your thoughts because if your loved ones know your battles, they just may walk out.

So, you're in hiding, incognito, not in touch with yourself. If you aren't sure who you are, how do you expect someone else?

It's clammy and cold in the trenches of doubt. How will you ever cope? I know you're still trying to figure that out.

Just tired of being the same after constantly trying to change. Tired of living in fear, worrying about what the future may bring.

Who Am I? What Am I? Why Am I here? What's the reason for the struggle? Pain can't be a career?

What to do? Where to Go? How will I know when I'm there? These are questions many ask when they are crying in prayer.

So far out, not content, but your faith keeps saying Hold on. I know that this time I'll make it cause the relationships strong.

Where are you? Do you hear me? Will you soon talk to me? Is this examination time? If so, I'll work quietly.

Not complaining, wandering, erasing doubt, fear, and hate. If those things continue to weigh you down, then you can't graduate.

I know my time is almost here because the battle is fierce. I know that I will overcome. That's the reason Jesus was pierced.

Commencement is imminent, and soon you'll be one step closer. You'll finally hear "Well Done, My Child. Aren't you glad the struggles are over?"

As you grab your diploma, there are no tears, only smiles. Freedom only feels good when you've been bound for a while.

Your heart is pumping, and your legs are jumping. This was well worth the wait. After all that you've been through, you can now celebrate.

Scriptures to meditate on: Psalm 23:4 NIV: "Even though I walk through the darkest valley, I will fear no evil, for you are with me; your rod and your staff they comfort me." King David understood the powerful concept of walking through a wilderness and stormy situations. He understood that he was just passing through. The valley of death was not his end, just a tunnel to get him to his next destination.

1 Corinthians 10:13 NIV, "No temptation has overtaken you except what is common to mankind. And God is faithful; he will not let you be tempted beyond what you can bear. But when you are tempted, he will also provide a way out so that you can endure it." The word of God lets us know that what we are experiencing is common; we must go through it. You will have to make a choice, though. Will you allow the temptation, trial, or test to consume you? Or will you

understand that God is in control, and you are just passing through? Will you trust him?

Reminders: Trusting God doesn't mean the storm will not come your way, but it does mean that you will be able to face it and overcome it. The flesh is weak and would rather give in and succumb than go through. You've got to deny your flesh. I know it's easier said than done, but it is imperative if you are going to make it through.

You belong to God. No matter what you've done, how you've strayed, or what temptations and tests you haven't passed. God loves you so much that he wants to give you the opportunity to make it through. He wants you. He wants your time. He wants your energy. He wants your love. God is a jealous God and knows how to get your attention.

Don't allow your flesh to keep you hindered. It will be a daily battle as you journey through the wilderness, but you can make it through. Moment by moment, day by day, one step at a time. Walk in the newness of life, go on through the wilderness knowing that you are just passing through, and this too shall pass. Victory will be coming after a while.

Chapter 36: Celebrate your Victories

Sometimes people are only looking at the big picture or the big dreams and visions and feel like if they are not influencing the world that they are not bringing change. This couldn't be further from the truth.

I believe when we dream about what our future is going to look like, we often see the end from the beginning. God gives this unbelievable glimpse, and we can become frightened by it or try to get there as fast as we can. I want to encourage you to take time to smell the flowers around you and celebrate every success, no matter how small. Celebrate the people that are in your path, whether they make the cut for a few months, a season, or for a lifetime, and most importantly, celebrate yourself.

I am a goal-driven person, so I usually don't celebrate small things until I've accomplished the task at hand. Until one day, I realized the small things are indeed the big things. For instance, in college, I was getting A's (and B's) on assignments left and right. I should've celebrated, but I was too focused on the next class, too focused on finishing and getting my degree (with some kind of laude at the end), that I missed some wonderful opportunities to celebrate myself and my accomplishments. When the big day came to commence, I felt this extreme load fall from my body, but that was a weight I was never designed to carry. I said to myself, never again. I will not wait to celebrate an accomplishment or a goal, even if I've got to celebrate alone. I became more intentional in celebrating every victory and not being hung up on failures.

I want to encourage you to enjoy your journey. Why? Because the journey is almost going to be as exciting and as rewarding as arriving. There are going to be obstacles, as we know all too well, but if you are only focused on getting to the top, you are going to miss a few steps that could really ground you and ensure you are ready for all that you've prayed for, worked for, and sought after. Pay attention to your surroundings, discern who's for you, who's just along for the ride, and who could really care less.

You can do it. If God has given you the vision, he has already equipped you with the gifts, the talent, the knowledge, the insight, and the wisdom. All you've got to do is tap into the energy and creativity you possess, believe in your heart, and never give up. Activate your faith, even if all you have is a little bit. I believe we've all seen God do a lot out of nothing. The word says if you have faith like a mustard seed (Matthew 17:20), nothing will be impossible to you.

There is someone who needs to hear from you.... Now! You matter, what you've gone through matters, what you've grown through matters, and your voice matters. It's time to manifest your dreams and watch them grow into fruition.

God is asking that you make the most of your time and the opportunities that he has given you. You are here to fulfill a task and complete the specific assignment that God has for you. There is so much that God wants to do in and for the lives of his people. However, to move and have free rein in our lives, God requires your trust in him.

Many a person has come to earth and left here without fully realizing what God wanted to do in their lives. Or worse, having a glimpse of what God wanted to do but allowed fear of people or negative thought patterns to keep them from experiencing the fullness and leaving their mark, no matter how great or small on this earth.

What will your payment be to get where you need to be in this life? Will you be disciplined? Will you stop listening to the voices that say you can't do it? Will you be focused? You must give up something to protect the vision, protect your time, and live the life that God's ordained for you. You can no longer sit on the sidelines and be normal.

You will need to trust, yield, and surrender to God. Feed your faith, starve your doubts, tell fear it must flee; there will be no place for it. Remember, you will never fit in when God has called you to stand out.

This is a time of stepping out and following the prompting and leading of the Holy Spirit. This is not a time to shrink back in fear or self-doubt, nor is it a time to quit.

The voices in your head may try to discourage you, but you have come too far, God has been too good, and you have too many people depending on you to rise and fulfill your destiny. Get alone with God, do what you must do to get yourself in focus, and prepare for your Now.

As you prepare for this level of going higher, don't worry about your age, your background, your story, or your lack of qualifications for what God is calling you to do. Our destinies may not include touching millions of lives, but there are more than a few people out there who are going to be impacted by your story, your vision, and your dream. My prayer for you is that you reach your destiny. Rest in the knowledge that God has chosen you, he has equipped you, and he has a plan for you.

Let these words encourage you and speak life to you. Know that God wants to heal you every place you hurt if only you give him the opportunity to. God wants you freed from demonic oppression, from mental stress and panic attacks, and in your physical health. You don't have to wait to die and go to heaven to enjoy heaven on earth. Jesus' message was the Kingdom of God, and he wants us to experience the Kingdom of God on earth as it is experienced in heaven. Take your dominion back over your life, your health, your family, your finances, and any other situation where fear and doubt have tried to creep in. God's best is reserved for you; start enjoying it now.

Chapter 37: I'm Proud of You

I am proud of you, yep, all of you who let go of one-sided friendships!

You know, the ones where you were only called on when they needed a ride, money, food, clothes, or had nobody else to hang with, so they chose you.

You know, the ones when you stopped giving into what they wanted, they stopped calling.

The ones you celebrated and prayed for when they were winning or down, but when it was your time to win, they were nowhere to be found. When you were down, they were nowhere around.

I am proud of you, proud of you for not changing who you are but setting boundaries on what you'll allow.

I'm proud that you didn't let their pity and lies continually drag you down.

Proud that you recognized the trend and started backing away so it wouldn't happen again.

I am proud of you, yep you!

When you got done wrong, and they tried to lie and slander your name, say all the things you did but never acknowledged any of their blame. Mad at you because you couldn't do for them one day. Forgetting the hundred times that you helped their family. Mad that you started to choose you first, upset that they couldn't continue to cause you to hurt.

Their happiness was comprised of bringing you down. Since you graduated with some discernment, you started recognizing the clowns.

Take, take, take, surrounded you, so you gave, and you gave.

Then God woke you up to tell you, "You are not a slave."

Not a slave to your emotions, to people, to yourself, or to your past.

You started changing your thoughts about yourself and stopped allowing the "usury" to last.

You got tired of being flattered in your face to later find you were dragged in the mud behind your back.

Tired of holding on to the guilt and the shame, no longer holding on to the pain and the blame.

You had to cut off the people who were no longer good for you.

Finally walking with your head up high, I'm proud of you, yep you!